DURHAM CITY
IN
50
BUILDINGS

DEREK DODDS

AMBERLEY

First published 2019

Amberley Publishing, The Hill, Stroud
Gloucestershire GL5 4EP

www.amberley-books.com

British Library Cataloguing in Publication Data.
A catalogue record for this book is available from the British Library.

ISBN 978 1 4456 8756 8 (print)
ISBN 978 1 4456 8757 5 (ebook)

Typesetting by Aura Technology and Software Services, India.
Printed in Great Britain.

Contents

Map   4

Key   6

Introduction   7

The 50 Buildings   9

Bibliography   95

Acknowledgements   96

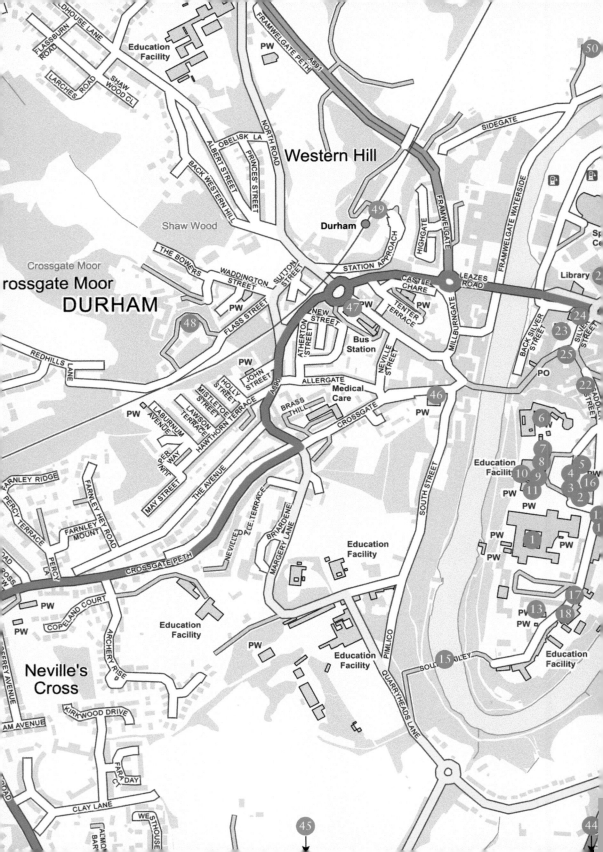

Key

1. Durham Cathedral
2. Abbey House
3. Pemberton Building
4. Bishop Cosin's Almshouses
5. Cosin's Hall
6. Durham Castle
7. Exchequer Building
8. Cosin's Library
9. University Library and former Registry Building
10. The Pace Extension
11. Divinity House Music School
12. St Mary-le-Bow
13. St Mary-the-Less
14. St Chad's College
15. Prebends' Bridge
16. Assembly Rooms
17. Haughton House
18. Bowes House
19. Hatfield College
20. Dunelm House
21. Kingsgate Bridge
22. Former Saddler Street Post Office
23. Town Hall and Guildhall
24. St Nicholas' Church
25. Former National Provincial Bank
26. The Gala Theatre and Cinema
27. Former United Reformed Church
28. St Antony's Priory
29. Leazes Place
30. Former Mechanics' Institute
31. Kepier House
32. Kepier Hospital
33. St Giles' Church
34. Vane Tempest Hall
35. Masonic Hall
36. Former Shire Hall
37. Elvet Methodist Church
38. Former Assize Courts
39. St Cuthbert's RC Church
40. Hallgarth Barns
41. Victoria Inn Public House
42. St Oswald's Church
43. The Palatine Centre
44. The Ogden Building
45. St Aidan's College
46. St Margaret's of Antioch
47. North Road Methodist Church
48. Redhills Miners' Hall
49. Durham Railway Station
50. Crook Hall

Introduction

Durham City has an embarrassment of architectural riches. Packed into a relatively small central area, some 600 of its buildings are listed, forty-one at Grade I. Yet officially rated or not, iconic or perhaps less so, the fifty included here reflect aspects of the remarkable history, culture and identity of this special place. Historic and modern, they are personal choices, which of course will not all be agreed with. Where relevant I have summarised entries from Historic England's listed buildings register but rather than providing a separate glossary, have attempted to explain some architectural terms in the text. Hopefully this helps the reader as much as it has helped me.

The architectural journey through Durham begins on Palace Green. At this high point of the peninsula, on an already sacred site, the majestic Romanesque cathedral was begun by the Normans in 1093 shortly after they had consolidated their rule with the powerful castle built nearby. From this stronghold and in their role as guardians of the north, Durham's Prince Bishops proceeded to develop their Palace Green enclave and exercise their jurisdiction over the medieval walled town and the boroughs which grew below it. A number of the bishops' impressive stone-built ventures, mainly parish churches, feature in this book.

Durham's building fabric suffered in post-medieval times. Damaged during the Civil War and neglected after the bishopric's abolition in 1646, major city buildings were saved by the restoration of the monarchy and the return to Durham of former prebend John Cosin. Between 1660 and 1672 he instigated rebuilding and restoration around Palace Green and in the city beyond. One of Durham's greatest Prince Bishops, his architectural influence remains impossible to ignore.

Durham's growth was sluggish during the episcopacies of Cosin's successors and comparatively slow afterwards. Contained by its narrow river loop on the peninsula, in Framwellgate to the west, the Elvets to the east and in a ribbon of development towards Gilesgate, the city's population reached barely 16,000 by the end of Victoria's reign. With only a few home-grown manufacturers, Durham never became an industrial hub like some of its booming regional neighbours. Politically reformed and given an extended franchise by the Municipal Corporations Act of 1835 however (shortly before the death of the last Prince Bishop), Durham City continued as an important ecclesiastical, judicial and administrative authority. Fine civic buildings, domestic properties, new churches and institutions from this lengthy historical time span are amongst the buildings illustrated here. Similarly, examples of Georgian elegance from the gentrified former castle baileys are shown.

Above: Durham's awe-inspiring cathedral viewed from the south-west on Observatory Hill.

Left: Durham Castle from Crossgate with St Margaret's Church tower in the right foreground.

Growth in Durham has accelerated over the last half century however, with education playing a significant part. Established on Palace Green in 1832, Durham University has undergone extraordinary expansion, particularly in recent decades. Campus enlargements just south of the river meander have added to the university's impressive estate and increased the numbers of distinguished architects who have worked in the city. Student numbers have surged and new accommodation for them has been constructed citywide. Yet transcending all, Durham's historic peninsula core seems unmoved. Crowned by cathedral and castle, this World Heritage Site has a reassuring permanence in the restless surrounding landscape.

The 50 Buildings

1. Durham Cathedral

'The Cathedral Church of Christ and St Mary the Virgin' straddles the southern tip of Durham's rocky peninsula and dominates its history. Construction of this huge Norman building commenced in 1093 and like the Anglo-Saxon structure that preceded it, the spiritual focus of the new cathedral and the city which grew around it was St Cuthbert, whose coffin found shelter at Durham in 995 and can be seen there today.

Almost every trace of the peninsula's earlier Northumbrian church was swept away and its replacement began to take shape. By 1133, through the vision and patronage of Norman bishops William St Calais and Ranulf Flambard, much of their new cathedral (apart from the western towers) appeared as it does today from Palace Green.

It followed the pattern of large-scale cathedrals established in England after 1066 which adopted the Christian cross or 'cruciform' floor plan. Durham was built on an east–west alignment with the high altar at the east end and the main doorway (afterwards moved) to the west. Between them is the 'crossing' where the arms of the symbolic cross stretch out, and above that is a soaring central tower. Built in stages, it was completed in the late fifteenth century and is over 200 feet high.

Durham is essentially a Romanesque cathedral. This architectural style, gaining popularity in Europe at the end of the first millennium AD, was inspired by ambitious Byzantine imperial structures and much later was associated with the classical buildings of ancient Rome. Their monumental appearance, conveying a powerful sense of order and strength, is loudly echoed at Durham. Obvious from the outside, this impression becomes subtler within its pale sandstone walls.

Although in fact shorter than some other Norman cathedrals, Durham's nave is nevertheless 201 feet long. Within this considerable space, originally intended by William St Calais to equal the Old St Peter's basilica in Rome, a procession of supporting piers combine massiveness with grace. They are regularly spaced and after the compound pairs at the west of the building, alternate between circular and compound (or 'clustered') shafts. Carved decoration on the round columns is a significant architectural innovation and one of the cathedral's major delights. (Incredibly done in the mason's yard before careful on-site positioning.) Where previously such effects were painted or comparatively small-scale carvings, fluted, lozenge, spiral and chevron (or 'zigzag') patterns were boldly incised into

Durham's circular piers, softening what would have been a permanently austere appearance. And they are also an integral part of the cathedral's parallel arcades.

Above them, common to other English churches, rises a 'triforium' or galleried arcade and a top-level clerestory where numerous windows help illuminate the building. Round arches and zigzag decoration of the upper tiers consolidate the Romanesque theme and Durham's examples are wide-bodied and purposeful with unusually balanced and 'pleasing' proportions. Their relationship to the rest of the nave is perfectly judged, achieving a harmony rarely surpassed.

Literally above everything however are Durham's high stone vaults, another classically Romanesque feature. Spanning wide spaces with fireproof stone instead of timber was always a challenge, but at Durham it became an architectural triumph. Building experimentation and advances in technique bore fruit at Durham and it became the first substantial English church to be fully vaulted with stone. Moreover, ribbed vaulting made one of its earliest European appearances in Durham. Long and slender skeletal-like stone ribs link the structure's disparate body parts. They reinforce the building's unity and strength and add lightness and finesse, pointing the way to a subsequent Gothic style. They can be best appreciated from the Choir aisles.

Two chapels, the Galilee and Nine Altars, were significant additions after the cathedral's initial building phase. Built at the west end, after failed attempts

Cathedral Cloister Garth and the west end Galilee Towers. (Basin from the refectory lavatorium in right foreground.)

Cathedral North Door and Central Lantern Tower above on the left.

at the structurally unstable east, Bishop Pudsey's new chapel was consecrated around 1175. Although having a Virgin Mary altar, it was probably originally intended to be dedicated to her as a Lady Chapel but became known instead as a Galilee, usually placed at the west to signify the final journey of Jesus through the Holy Land.

Dissimilar to the rest of the cathedral, the Galilee Chapel marks a clear transition between architectural styles. Romanesque and Gothic influences stand together, with round arches and crisp chevron decoration contrasted by slender piers with late Norman 'waterleaf' capitals. Its five-bay width matches the rest of the cathedral and contains the remnants of St Bede's once gilded shrine and the tomb chest of Bishop Langley, who restored the chapel before he died in 1437.

To address the problem of an appropriate replacement for the St Cuthbert's crumbling shrine (cramped into a semicircular east chapel or 'apse' behind the high altar since 1104), the Chapel of the Nine Altars was finally constructed in the late 1270s. Particularly deep foundations and 7-feet-thick walls overcame the east end's geological problems and the new chapel consolidated Durham as an important site of medieval pilgrimage.

Located across the huge back wall of the chapel, nine altars dedicated to individual saints allowed more masses to be said. Several feet lower than the main building's adjacent choir, the new chapel was influenced by Fountain's Abbey and with its tall lancet windows and slim columns, shares the Early English Gothic styling of this Yorkshire contemporary. Notable for a magnificent rose window, Durham's Nine Altars Chapel makes extensive use of local Frosterley 'marble' and contains fine sculpture, particularly in the vaulting. Cuthbert's shrine itself, 6 feet above the chapel floor, was said before the Reformation to be 'of marble and gold, with an enormous emerald'. Even without the medieval glitter, the saint's tomb continues to be a centre of attraction. It is an extraordinary place in an extraordinary building.

The monastic buildings adjoining the cathedral, especially the fourteenth-century Monk's Dormitory and Prior's Kitchen, are similarly outstanding. Now housing the 'Open Treasure' exhibition, opened in 2016 and designed by Purcell architects, the dormitory has a spectacular oak-beamed roof and the Great Kitchen has distinctive vaulting. Now containing relics of St Cuthbert, they are well worth visiting and make an impressive contribution to what was recognised by the Institute of British Architects in 1984 as the 'best building in the world'.

2. Abbey House

Standing opposite the cathedral, Abbey House occupies the south-east corner of Palace Green, extending down the slope of Dun Cow Lane and incorporating the former Abbey Cottage.

A simple but well-balanced five-bay front of sandstone ashlar is stepped back from neighbours on the Green and its full Georgian symmetry was revealed during renovations in 1973 when two windows on the top floor were unblocked. Beyond this are even older structures. A typically late seventeenth-century Dutch gable with Flemish Bond brickwork can be glimpsed above the Dun Cow Lane elevation where at ground level an exposed section of ancient stonework adds to the building's intriguing complexity. A section of pebble-dash rendering was removed during early 1970s refurbishment and extension work (overseen by Cambridge-based architect David Roberts), uncovering what is interpreted as a remnant of the first Abbey House. A blocked arched door and what are believed to be stairway fragments, confidently dated to the twelfth century, indicate that the house then faced the cathedral and Lychgate, on the site of today's Dun Cow Lane. The original house was probably amongst several tenement properties (including its immediate neighbour Abbey Cottage) clustering near the castle and Palace Green's protective walls, which were built during the episcopate of Bishop Flambard (1099–1128) and afterwards extended down to the River Wear at Kingsgate. For centuries the area was in the hands of Durham's Prince Bishops and reasonably comprehensive cathedral archives list many occupants of Abbey House and its neighbours, from Will Wermouth in 1395 to lawyer R. Burrell after 1804. Most of the tenants appear to be officials who served the bishop and later the Dean and Chapter of Durham.

Above: Abbey House, at the corner of Palace Green and Dun Cow Lane.

Right: Dutch Gable (above) and blocked medieval arch (below) on the south side of Abbey House.

By around 1720, when architecture was more domestic than defensive, a stylish new façade was added and Abbey House was transformed into a fine town house facing squarely across Palace Green. Sturdy gate piers and railings were added but these were uprooted in the twentieth century, leaving the low stone plinths seen today. A handsome doorcase with carved acanthus leaf brackets survives intact however, and a few interior features, notably an ornately carved Restoration period staircase and elegant Georgian paneling, remain as reminders of a gracious past. Abbey House began a new life in 1899 when it was used as accommodation for Durham's first female students. Afterwards it became St Mary's Women's College and in the 1960s was student accommodation for University College. Now it is used to teach theology and religion.

3. Pemberton Building

Deliberately intended to appear old, the Pemberton Building is in fact a relatively new addition to Palace Green. Separated from Abbey House by the narrowest of alleys, the Pemberton (also known as the Pemberton Rooms) was opened in 1931, replacing demolished stables and a small cottage. Built to house university lecture rooms, it was designed by architect W. D. Caroe in predominantly neo-Tudor style.

Of Danish extraction, Caroe was born near Liverpool in 1857 and specialised in the restoration of ecclesiastical architecture as well as educational buildings. (His firm, founded in 1884, remains in operation.) Above all however Caroe became a major figure in Victorian Britain's Arts and Crafts movement, an influence seen in his work on Palace Green. Admiration for pre-industrial buildings and the craftsmanship that created them was at the heart of Arts and Crafts philosophy, but Caroe was also open to other styles. Gabled dormers and tall windows with leaded glass are amongst many Tudor influences on the Pemberton Building, but the battlements on the left-hand tower owe something to Norman architecture while shaped gables on the right are echoes of the adjacent Abbey House.

'Snecked' or randomly sized blocks have been used widely in the building's construction, producing a hand-finished look, which gives an antique effect and emphasises the mason's highly prized individual skill. Similarly meticulous workmanship is on show throughout, from the finely detailed stone plaques and friezes above the arched Tudoresque entrance, to the iron-framed and chamfered wood panels of impressive front doors. Inside, simple but hefty stone pillars and the staircase would not look too out of place in the nearby castle or the cathedral. A sweepingly curved balustrade reflects the early twentieth-century taste for art nouveau.

Façade of Pemberton Building with Almshouses on left.

Pre-Pemberton old Buildings between Almshouses and Abbey House on Palace Green. (Gibby Collection, reproduced by kind permission of Durham University Library)

Yet Caroe's eclectic attempt to sympathetically reflect Palace Green's wide range of historic buildings has been met with lukewarm praise. Pevsner wrote of the Pemberton's 'Cold, grey stone', an opinion restated by Durham architectural expert Martin Roberts in his latest work. Yet Roberts also acknowledges the dash of interest added to the Durham scene by the Pemberton Buildings and the respect that Caroe's design has for its eminent neighbours on Palace Green.

Named in honour of John Stapleton Grey Pemberton (1860–1940), President of Durham College Council, the Pemberton Rooms remain as lecture theatres and also host lively debates sponsored by the university's historic Durham Union Society.

4. Bishop Cosin's Almshouses

Cosin's Almshouses are part of an important group of historic buildings built by one of Durham's most significant Prince Bishops. Squatting at the centre of Palace Green's eastern side, this sandstone and ashlar structure was built in 1666, replacing the music and grammar schools erected by Bishop Langley over two centuries before and burned by the Scots in 1640. Intended to relieve local poverty and distress, almshouses were first established in England during the tenth century and Bishop Cosin had already built one at Bishop Auckland in 1662.

Cosin's new two-storey structure in Durham City comprised, in fact, of three buildings, with new Grammar and Song Schools at the north and south wings flanking Cosin's Almshouses in the middle. All of them are by the hand of John Langstaffe, Cosin's master mason-cum-architect. Langstaffe, a Bishop Auckland man, was obviously highly regarded by the High Church Cosin, who retained the builder's services despite his Quaker beliefs.

In a surviving ink plan by Langstaffe, the almshouses are shown as a work in progress. The 'bookend' gabled schools on the left and right were retained and a slightly modified window arrangement was included in the finished building. More significantly however, designs for a sophisticated and classically styled doorcase were abandoned in favour of the traditional and more sober Tudor arched version seen today. John Cosin's generally conservative view of architecture had won out and the Prince Bishop sealed his approval with his crest and coat of arms above the almshouses' Tudor arched doorway.

A lengthy charter of conditions, written and signed by Cosin himself, strictly regulated almshouse life. Each of the often elderly or infirm inhabitants, four women and four men, were allocated single rooms in Palace Green's newly opened charitable institution. To qualify for entry, they had to be unmarried, of good character (sometimes termed 'the respectable poor') and be from Durham City or nearby Brancepeth, where Cosin had served as rector. They were expected not to gamble or visit taverns, to follow a programme of individual prayer in the almshouse and were provided with uniforms for their daily processions across Palace Green to cathedral services. Presumably there was no shortage of

HOSPITALE EPĪ DUNELM
PRO VIII PAUPERIBUS
FUNDAT PER JOH EPISCOP
A·D· MDCLXVI

Above: Almshouse building with its main roof under repair. The doorway to the Pemberton Rooms is seen on the far right.

Left: Cosin's coat of arms above the central Almshouse door. Bishop Langley's crest (a star and six bars) remains just identifiable on the building's north and south gables.

almshouse applicants however, as in addition to food and lodging, each inmate was granted eight pounds one shilling and fourpence annually. This benefit came from a £70 annuity, raised on land outside Durham City that Cosin purchased from his private funds.

Cosin's Almshouses remained in use until 1837, when they were taken over by the university for student lodgings. Afterwards the interior was heavily altered to house the university museum's taxidermy, herbarium and historical artefacts collection. Restored by William Caroe in conjunction with building the Pemberton next door, the almshouses are presently shared by university security staff and a restaurant business.

5. Cosin's Hall

Formerly 'Archdeacon's Inn' but now named after the seventeenth-century bishop, 'Cosin's Hall' stands at the north-eastern entrance to Palace Green. Grade II* listed since 1952, this seven-bay three-storey eye-catcher was amongst Durham's first predominantly brick structures built at a time when timber and stone were becoming less favoured. A typically well-balanced Georgian façade (despite an oddly off-centre entrance, suggested by Alec Clifton-Taylor to be a 'provincial' design) dates the mansion to around 1700, but it may well have been a restoration then and has certainly been altered since. A possibly embellished cornice across the top of the building has been removed and stuccoed lintels and decoratively curved ledges replace original window brickwork. Similarly, sections of the building have been obviously reworked, indicated by colour variations in brick courses and patched in areas of older masonry, particularly at ground-floor level on the northern side.

Yet the hall's crowning glory has been comparatively untouched. At the top of a short flight of stairs, the impressive doorcase was obviously intended to assure visitors they were entering a building of quality. Framed by Ionic pilasters and topped by an arched hood is an intricately carved seashell, a characteristically Rococo motif fashionable during the eighteenth century. Carved around the shell is a swirl of foliage, a further display of flamboyant and highly decorative Rococo styling.

Unfortunately the early social history of this distinctive building is rather less apparent. A property deed from May 1456 refers to the archdeacon of Durham's 'hospicium' or place of hospitality in the castle's North Bailey adjacent to Palace Green. But what subsequently became called 'Archdeacon's Inn' is now better known for more modern associations with Durham University.

Cosin's Hall – a grand introduction to Palace Green.

Rococo finery on Cosin's Hall.

Shortly after it was established in 1832, the fledgling university rushed to place its first students into temporary lodgings at the old inn, naming it logically enough 'University House'. Between 1851 and 1864, as the university attempted to expand, the apparently run-down house served as Cosin's Hall college and afterwards adopted its present name. It was used for lectures and at the close of the nineteenth century also became a common room for St Cuthbert's Society, another Durham college.

Adaptation of Cosin's Hall for student use has continued and a further conversion for student accommodation was carried out in the 1990s. In 2006 the university's newly formed Institute of Advanced Study began work in Cosin's Hall and although unsurprisingly almost nothing of the original interior remains, this fine building provides a fitting location for such a prestigious organisation.

6. Durham Castle

The Normans stamped their authority on Durham with this building. Angered by the slaughter of a large Norman contingent and their commander by rebellious Northumbrians in the city a few years before, William the Conqueror ordered work to begin on a powerful new stronghold in 1072. What confronts the visitor today is a complex structure, built in various stages and styles over many centuries. Best appreciated from the northern side, it presents the classic profile of a heavily battlemented medieval fortification.

Laid out in typical Norman fashion, the castle's construction exploited the site's considerable natural defences and probably enhanced earlier Saxon ramparts. Raised high on an earthen mound or motte, a timber keep was built to guard the northern approaches to the city. Stone soon enclosed the wooden tower, while around the castle bailey to the west, further walls and steep-sided riverbanks made the site almost impregnable.

Of William's original castle, a crypt or 'Norman Chapel' (although an originally religious purpose has now been questioned) is believed to be a substantial remnant. Located in the courtyard at the edge of the present castle's northern range, this remarkable structure has been claimed by archaeologist Peter Clack to be perhaps the peninsula's 'most enchanting piece of Norman architecture'. Constructed from locally quarried veined sandstone with a largely intact herringbone-patterned floor, the diminutive building certainly has a serenity only equalled by areas of the nearby cathedral. A low vaulted ceiling is supported by rows of sandstone columns capped by sculpted human, animal and plant forms. Strange and primitively carved, it is easy to believe they might even be pre-Conquest survivors, but this dark and atmospheric space is more generally held to have been built in the decade or so following 1072, as Durham's Prince Bishops began their reign.

These men undoubtedly wielded great spiritual and secular power but in their ranks were also great builders who energised the development of a castle which became their palace as well as their fortress. Walcher, Bishop of Durham from 1072 to 1080, is credited with laying the foundations but his successors are largely responsible for the substantial castle buildings seen today.

On Palace Green, through the Norman arch of the Gatehouse (shifted there by Bishop Flambard around 1100 and 'Gothicised' by James Wyatt in 1791) there is a glimpse of the courtyard and splendid buildings beyond. On the left, approached by a palatial set of steps, is the late thirteenth-century Great Hall. It was built over a Norman undercroft by Anthony Bek, perhaps Durham's most aristocratic and martial Prince Bishop. Over 100 feet long and 45 feet high, this cavernous space rivals its Oxford and Cambridge counterparts. An oak-timbered roof dates from the era of Bishop Hatfield (1345–81) but Bek would recognise two windows on the hall's western side. Shorter than the rest, they have two lights and swirling geometrical tracery. A large kitchen block, necessary to supply the hall (and still in use today), was added by Bishop Fox in 1499. Converted from Norman chambers and possibly original kitchens to the rear of the hall, it has a pair of huge fireplaces. Looking like miniature castle ramparts, their chimney breasts are of brick, probably its first use in County Durham. They are indicative of the Bishops' wealth and the lavish hospitality dispensed by their court.

Linking the Great Hall complex on the west and the Norman range of the castle on the north, Bishop Cosin's renowned cantilever or 'flying' staircase (although subsequently propped with oak columns) provides a greater display of architectural finesse. Erected inside a new stair tower by this great Durham renovator in 1662, the elaborate woodcarving of the 'Black Stairs', as they are now known, was influential not only in Durham City but elsewhere in the country. Built to improve access and comfort in a cramped area of the medieval building, they lead on to the north range and more of the castle's finest Norman work.

Established by Flambard, the north range was rebuilt by Bishop Pudsey (1153–95) after a severe fire wrecked most of the locality. Two halls stacked on each other are believed to have been created and the so-called 'Norman Arch' and 'Norman Gallery' are magnificent survivors from that time. Compared by Pevsner to Durham Cathedral's finely carved cloister doorway, the archway was rediscovered during restoration work by Shute Barrington, Durham's penultimate Prince Bishop.

Concealed for centuries by lath and plaster, the late Norman arch is supported by three orders of columns and is profusely decorated with crisply cut geometric and naturalistic motifs. Above it in Pudsey's Upper Hall, the Norman Gallery is another impressive example of the stonemasons' craft. Once called the 'Constable's Hall', the lengthy gallery was reduced in width for university use but retains its Romanesque arcades and arches rich in chevron or 'zigzag' ornamentation.

Yet of all the bishops who built, altered and improved Durham Castle, Cuthbert Tunstall is said to have transformed it. During his turbulent reign from 1530 until 1559, 'Golden Old Man' Tunstall somehow managed to bring a modernising hand to a medieval and often impractical building. A new two-storey gallery was laid out across Pudsey's old north range, disguising (as well as buttressing) some of the starker Norman façade behind it and adding more than a touch of Tudor sophistication with elegant windows and doors. More importantly for Tunstall however, his fashionable gallery allowed easier progression between the Great Hall at one end and a new chapel at the other. Perhaps less enigmatic than the nearby Norman example, Tunstall's new chapel, extended by successive bishops, remains a richly furnished and distinctive space.

Spasmodic repair and restoration of the building (particularly by John Cosin and Nathaniel Crewe) continued until the time of William van Mildert, Durham's last Prince Bishop. Following his death in 1836, the castle embraced a rather different role as part of Durham's newly formed university and a reconstruction of

Bishop Cosin's eye-catching entrance to the Great Hall in Durham Castle.

Castle Clock and Bell Tower with Keep on right.

Durham Castle's extraordinary Norman Chapel.

the ruined keep by Anthony Salvin in 1841, creating a single staircase through the mound to the floors above, provided student lodgings. Restoration by C. Hodgson Fowler between 1877 and 1888 in the Great Hall and Tunstall Chapel was followed by far greater work however. Funded by substantial American donations in the remedial work in the early twentieth century, underpinning and other essential remedial work saved the castle from collapse. Carried out by W. T. Jones of Durham, the work was planned by consultant structural engineer Oscar Faber (1886–1956). This iconic castle has withstood the historic journey from Norman fortress to bishops' palace and now university use. It has embraced change and continues to be adapted and repaired for modern purposes.

7. Exchequer Building

Close by the castle gateway and sometimes overlooked, the Exchequer is a highly significant building. Part of the University Library since the 1850s and now refurbished, it is the last survivor of a range of medieval administrative buildings that were grouped around Palace Green.

Above: Exchequer Building with Cosin's Library on the left.

Left: Restored and repainted Neville arms (below) and Durham crest (above).

Built between around 1438 and 1457 for Bishop Robert Neville, the Exchequer (or Treasury) played an important part in the legal and financial business of the Durham diocese. Used to manage his considerable revenue and store his accounts, it was symbol of the Prince Bishop's power. It also had a cell for those falling foul of the palatinate court and apparently replaced earlier buildings. A document referring to the west side of Palace Green in 1388 mentions 'houses' which contained the 'Chancery, Exchequer, Receipt and a hall for the Pleas of Justice'.

Nevilles' three-storey Exchequer has two bays and was built from Durham's 'golden' sandstone. Late medieval double lancets remain on the weighty north façade but dark coping stones on the parapet were nineteenth-century replacements for a previously battlemented roof.

Restoration of the structure was carried out by Bishop Cosin as part of his rejuvenation of Palace Green after he returned to Durham in August 1661. (He had been a prebend there between 1624 and 1643.) Despite approaching seventy, the new Prince Bishop employed remarkable energy in rebuilding an area of the city badly affected by both Scottish occupations during the Civil War. A great improver and capable of grand architectural ideas, John Cosin was actively involved in the building process as well as the planning. But as hinted at by his repaired Exchequer, he could also be bound by his respect for order and tradition. While larger than their predecessors, the main façade windows, replaced by Cosin in 1688 (and renewed in the nineteenth century), were originally unfashionable.

The Exchequer was built just outside the medieval castle's barbican at the edge of its dry moat. Its ground floor is below the level of Palace Green, reached by stairs down to a studded door framed by a Tudor surround. Although the interior is greatly changed, original ceiling beams and newel stairs survive. A genuine medieval treasure, the Exchequer is set to be opened for occasional public tours.

8. Cosin's Library

Amongst John Cosin's building projects on Palace Green, the library was closest to his heart. Scholarship and the love of learning underpinned the life of this intellectual prelate and his book collection was renowned. During his exile in Paris it is suggested he would rather buy a book than a loaf of bread.

Unsurprisingly then, building costs for his new library were only a fraction of the £2,000 lavished on extra volumes to furnish its shelves. Cosin again turned to his preferred local builder John Langstaffe, who carried out the work between 1667 and 1668. Like the Exchequer Building it adjoins, the library was originally battlemented and also shares similar round-arched windows on the main façade.

As always, Bishop Cosin was particular about the specification and design of his latest enterprise. He called for higher-grade local sandstone to be used and an architectural model was made for him, since sadly lost. Not only a repository for his impressive book collection, the new building was also intended to be Durham's 'great Publick Library'. For Cosin and his elite contemporaries however, it was a public composed of scholars and gentlemen only.

While it was certainly inspired by examples in Paris and Madrid, the Durham structure is described by Cosin scholar Adrian Green as 'astylar' – constructed without the classical columns and pilasters that distinguished those grander European libraries. But a baroque central doorway and broken pediment, with the Bishop's blue and gold regalia above it, gave a measure of elegance to Cosin's own episcopal library, which opened in 1669.

Above: Cosin's heraldic arms and inscription above library door.

Left: Cosin's Library flanked by main library building on the left and Exchequer building on the right.

Below: Interior of Cosin's Library. (Image courtesy of Durham University Library)

Although some original style was blunted in the 1830s when Anthony Salvin added the exterior Gothic tower or oriel and the crenellations were removed, the library's interior has remained a showy place. The main hall, over 50 feet long, 30 feet wide and 26 feet high, is lined by bookcases interspersed with smaller bays, originally designed as reading spaces but quickly filled with more shelves. Tiny 'dentils' – tooth-shape decoration – ornament the large bookcase cornices, while the niches between are embellished with fruit-laden swags and motifs incorporating Cosin's insignia. Portrait roundels of classical historians, philosophers and poets watch over the double book bookcases, a guide to what may be found below.

Yet even all this was not enough to contain Cosin's swelling collection and in 1671 Langstaffe squeezed in an extension, now known as 'Little Cosin', between the library and the Exchequer Building. Further improvements, including an internal gallery and Tudoresque fireplace, followed university administration in 1832. Cosin's heartfelt Latin motto however still remains above his library door. Translated it reads, 'Not the least part of education is to be acquainted with good books.'

9. University Library and Old Registry

Building upon Cosin's substantial collection, Durham University Library has steadily expanded along the west side of Palace Green. It had the best of starts with Cosin's books, augmented by another 160 from Bishop Van Mildert in 1833 following the university's inauguration. More importantly perhaps, Van Mildert also gifted a variety of Dean and Chapter property, which formed the backbone of today's flourishing library institution.

Initially, various Palace Green stable blocks were modified to serve as Maths and Greek lecture rooms before they were demolished in 1882 and replaced by the present two-storey structure. It was built by Sir Arthur Blomfield (1829–99) in a 'perpendicular' or late English Gothic style, which emphasises the vertical elements of this tall building's windows and the ecclesiastical like tracery within them. Viewed in isolation, Blomfield's Palace Green work has echoes of the many churches he either built or restored during the Victorian 'craze' for Gothic Revival architecture. The library's main entrance however, reverting to a more solid classicism, boasts an imposing porch with Tuscan columns, erected in the mid-1930s by renowned architectural practice Caröe and Passmore.

Blomfield's building, in library use since 1929, has since undergone extensive modification and expansion, providing purpose-built exhibition spaces and research rooms as well as housing the university's special collections. Yet perhaps one of its most interesting acquisitions was the adjacent Old Registry, incorporated into the library in 1978.

Above: Sir Arthur Blomfield's main library building with Cosin's Library on right and former Registry on left.

Left: The Old Registry, built on the site of Palace Green's seventeenth-century County Court House. The right-hand doorway may be a remnant of that building.

This interesting building, its southern corner resting on the Windy Gap vennel, dates from 1820 and was the registry for the Durham diocese. It supported the bishop with legal advice, stored bishopric records and handled a bewildering range of administrative issues, from probate matters to marriage licence applications. All this was carried out in a crenellated building with buttresses that give it a fortress-like appearance. Built by an unknown architect for Bishop Shute Barrington, this single-storey seven-bay edifice is of sandstone and ashlar construction and has been

Grade II listed since 1952. Formerly used by the Durham Union Society, it stands on the site of the County Court, rebuilt by Bishop Cosin in 1644 and demolished in 1811. Had that structure survived, its Italianate arched stone arcade, or 'loggia', might have made it the most remarkable building on Palace Green.

1C. The Pace Extension

Of all the alterations and additions to the library complex on Palace Green, none have been as radical as the Pace extension. York-based George Pace knew Durham well. Appointed consultant architect to the cathedral in 1954 and undertaking university projects since 1958, he was commissioned to extend the Palace Green arts library in 1961. Successfully setting his grand design into Durham's internationally acclaimed landscape, between castle and cathedral, was a daunting task. But when the building was completed in 1966, Pace had achieved even more than that.

Built behind the main library, largely out of sight of Palace Green and overlooking the river, Pace's startling construction is five storeys high. Occupying the site of an old garden, his stone-walled building is supported by a concrete framework, its façades a careful juxtaposition of smoothly ordered ashlar and wildly irregular rubble blocks. Always sensitive to the precious historical environments he worked in, Pace used sandstones, both fine grained Dunhouse stone and locally sourced material. Unlike their traditionally coursed counterparts however, the rough-sawn rubble was laid without any pretence of deliberate order in a jagged, abstract appearance. Similarly, the library stair tower not only resembles a medieval bastion, but is placed alongside Windy Gap where one once stood.

This fusion of new and old was a keynote of his approach. Born in 1915, George Gaze Pace was inspired by the Arts and Crafts movement but embraced more modernist styles. A talented sketcher of churches, he was drawn to the work of William Morris, Rennie Mackintosh and later, Le Corbusier. Some of the library's internal arrangements are thought to have been influenced by Mackintosh and the reading room's geometric lightwells have strong Le Corbusier overtones. Meticulous attention to detail was another Pace trademark. During the building process, exposed workings were always covered by polythene and a protective limewash was applied to all newly erected stone walls.

While the Pace library has been hailed by Martin Roberts as a 'triumph', there have been some detractors. Pevsner found it 'disappointing' and 'fidgety' and in the early days it was seen locally as slightly 'intrusive'. (Subsequently withdrawn when its height was reduced.) Nevertheless, it may be an overstatement to call it a masterpiece, but after half a century the Pace Library has earned its place amongst Durham's landmark buildings.

Above: Pace Building's main façade overlooking the River Wear.

Left: Library's interior lighting scheme. (Author's image with the permission of Durham University Library)

11. Divinity House Music School

Occupying the south-west corner of Palace Green, this 'L' shaped structure began life as a grammar school in 1541, possibly on the foundations of a medieval tithe barn. The school was rebuilt at the beginning of Bishop Cosin's episcopate in 1661, and though the building's east end wall is dominated by a characteristically large 'Cosin' window, the school was planned by the cathedral's Dean and Chapter over which Bishop Cosin had limited control.

Above: Divinity House – schoolroom on the right, master's house on the left.

Right: Restored 'Cosin' window at the east end of Divinity House.

In his correspondence, he fretted over the new school's cost, size and the poor quality of its stonework. Nevertheless, the establishment moved forward under the tutelage of such men as Thomas Battersby, a Darlington headmaster, and Thomas Rudd, a Cambridge scholar. Their desks or 'thrones' surrounded by pupils, they taught in the building's single large schoolroom, its panelled walls a target for schoolboy graffiti which can still be seen.

A range of rooflines, window sizes and door styles indicate the evolution of a building extended and improved over the centuries. (Reused stone is particularly noticeable on the Windy Gap elevation.) The original one-storey school hall retains simple Tudor period door surrounds while the taller master's house to the west has another Tudor arch overlaid with an early eighteenth-century doorcase. Its wooden frame is decorated with a 'pulvinated' (or raised profile) frieze. Most prominent however are the old school hall's twin dormers, their original windows significantly enlarged by cathedral clerk of works George Pickering (probably advised by Anthony Salvin) in 1844.

That year also marked the end of an era at Durham Grammar School. Lack of space forced a move across the river to the present Quarryheads site and no longer would pupils have to use the cathedral graveyard as their playground.

Afterwards named 'Divinity House', the former school passed into university hands and a further extension, overlooking the river gorge, was added during Victorian times. This historic old grammar school was converted into the university's music department by the Bernard Taylor Partnership in 1966. Nowadays, instead of chanted Greek or Latin verse, classical music is often heard drifting across Palace Green.

12. St Mary-le-Bow

Little is known of this church before the collapse of its adjoining 'bow' or arched wall in August 1637. Historian Margot Jonson has suggested it was the 'Great St Mary's' attended in the twelfth century by St Godric and it is recorded that the early church had a tower with three bells.

It is more certain however that the tower became part of the city's defences, bonded into a wall built from the cathedral's east end, which divided the castle's outer bailey into north and south sectors. A gate between the two, shown on a 1595 drawing by Matthew Pattison, was castellated and pierced with a central round arch attached to the church bell tower. A few decades later and storm damaged by masonry from the fallen 'bow' gateway, St Mary's lay in partial ruins. Delayed by the Civil War, the parish church was eventually repaired and reopened in 1685, funded by contributions from the local gentry, the Dean and Chapter, and Nathaniel Lord Crewe, Bishop of Durham. To complete the project, the bell tower was restored in around 1702.

St Mary-le-Bow was reconstructed with some salvaged features. A medieval stone newel stair remains in the tower along with some two-light windows and a west-facing door. Although much of the remaining fabric dates from an 1875–76 restoration by university architect John Henry, some parapet battlements may be original, recalling St Mary's ancient link to Durham's walled citadel. Exterior stepped buttresses consolidate this martial effect and a three-bay nave, built on the slope of Bow Lane, narrows into a two-bay chancel. Victorian tracery on the perpendicular windows has been well executed (possibly by Ignatius Bonomi in 1843) and beyond them the church has a high-quality interior.

Above: St Mary-le-Bow seen from Durham's North Bailey.

Right: Rood screen in St Mary-le-Bow.

Turned into a museum in 1975, St Mary's interior has remained on show, nowhere more apparent than in its splendid rood screen, carved in 1707 with garlanded fruit and flower decoration. This is matched by stall ends and chancel panelling, of a slightly later date but in equally flourishing 'Cosin style'. Above the exterior west door there is an old blind arch, probably incorporated during the eighteenth-century rebuilding phase. It is a reminder of the fall and rise of St Mary-le-Bow.

13. St Mary-the-Less

Probably named as 'Little' or 'the Less' to differentiate it from nearby churches also dedicated to the Virgin Mary, St Mary's sits on a shoulder-high plot in Durham's South Bailey. Though small in stature, the church has prestigious historical connections. Founded by the Bulmers of Brancepeth in the early twelfth century, it was then patronised by their successors the Nevilles of Raby Castle.

At first glance, the round arch and chevron mouldings in the south porch might seem to confirm St Mary's Norman roots. Yet much of the building was reconstructed between 1846 and 1847. Apart from a single relocated window, some interior fragments of decoration and other reused materials, no original antiquities remain. Most in fact had disappeared before the wholesale rebuilding of a church described in Hutchinson's 1823 history as a 'mean edifice'.

Plans for its complete restoration were laid as early as 1780. A drawing by cathedral clerk of works George Nicholson illustrates a church that was never built. Fitted with box pews and with an apsidal east end, the projected structure reflected Georgian taste and Anglican ways of worship. Over half a century later, St Mary's took a different turn. Designed this time by George Pickering and doubtlessly advised by architect Anthony Salvin, the church was finally rebuilt in Romanesque Revival or 'neo-Norman' style. This was also influenced by historian and antiquarian James Raine, rector at St Mary's since 1828.

St Mary-the-Less from its South Bailey churchyard.

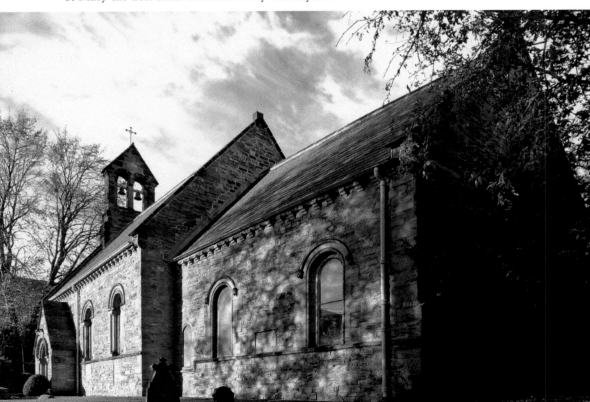

George Nicholson's
proposed redesign
of St Mary-the-Less.
(Drawing by
Andrew Dodds)

Believed to follow the original ground plan, the 'new' St Mary's remained faithful
to a traditional ashlar and squared sandstone build. It also restored an interior arch
between chancel and nave while on the west façade, a trio of bold round-headed
windows are framed with shafts and 'cushioned' capitals. Romanesque in style, they
are thought to have been inspired by the arcade in Durham Castle.

St Mary-the-Less has continued to change. It became St John's University chapel
in 1919 and has recently welcomed Durham's Orthodox Christian Community
into the congregation.

Contemporary English oak liturgical fittings, designed by Martin Grierson,
were a central focus of refurnishing carried out in 2002.

14. St Chad's College

Since opening on the peninsula in 1904, St Chad's College has expanded
to occupy a collection of Georgian houses in and around the North Bailey.
Contrasting and yet complementing them, the gently curving front of St Chad's
main building was constructed at the end of 1961. Built in mellow brick in
response to the ashlar of the facing cathedral, it contains an impressive dining
hall, kitchens and student accommodation. Said to resemble a bishop's mitre,
St Chad's unusual shape could also allude to its site on the corner of Bow Lane,
opposite the church of St Mary-le-Bow.

Above: St Chad's dining room.

Left: Curved front elevation of St Chad's.

Below: Rear view of St Chad's.

Replacing some buildings and converting others, St Chad's new development was designed by architect Francis Johnson (1911–95) who opened his Yorkshire practice in 1937. St Chad's was a most ambitious commission, finally overturning a more intrusive pre-war scheme proposed by London-based architect Leslie Thomas Moore.

Johnson's proposal was a clever solution to a complex problem. With the advice of Durham town planner Thomas Sharp, he provided a modern and spacious wing for St Chad's, which also preserved the bailey's Georgian integrity. The new building's height and width sit comfortably with its neighbours, while the main elevation, combining sash and rounded windows (with Gothic arched glazing bars), does not disturb the historic environment.

All of which accords well with Johnson's methods. Known to carefully research the historical context of his projects, he is now recognised as a significant figure in the urban conservation movement. St Chad's is an early demonstration of this. Aside from the new build on the bailey corner, Johnson's transformed four adjoining properties between 1961 and 1963. Saving their street frontages, he largely rebuilt or restored their backs, forming a gabled rear elevation which, although new, reflects the individuality and compatibility of the old houses beside it. Enough space was released for a neoclassical courtyard (later covered over) as well as common rooms for the increasing student population.

St Chad's foundation stone was laid on 15 December 1961 by the Bishop of Wakefield, John Ramsbotham. He was chairman of a governing body that developed St Chad's future plans and employed a visionary architect to carry them out.

15. Prebends' Bridge

Often regarded as the most gracious of Durham's historic river crossings, Prebends' Bridge spans the Wear to the south-west of the peninsula and was built by the cathedral Dean and Chapter for the convenience of their clergy and officials. Like many contemporaries it was erected after disastrous regional flooding in 1771. An abutment from Prebend's destroyed predecessor, which was built in 1696, still lies further upstream on the river's west bank.

Advised by London-based architect Robert Mylne, George Nicholson constructed the new bridge between August 1772 when the foundation stone was laid and 1778, when it was opened. Pleasantly symmetrical, the mainly squared sandstone and ashlar structure has a trio of semicircular arches 66 feet in diameter. They are neatly edged with 'voussoirs', wedge-like stones that give the arches shape as well as strength. Below them, two central river piers have triangular cutwaters or 'starlings', built from brick to divert the water flow. Angled hexagonal projections rise above the starlings, forming recessed bays on each of the walkway sides. Prime vantage points for cathedral and riverbank views, these once served as pedestrian shelters or passing places for horse-drawn traffic.

Now vehicle free (except in emergency), the bridge carriageway is 53 feet above the river and 22 feet wide. The parapet is plain with a thin cornice, but some sections of classical balustrading remain at each end, a stylistic feature no doubt admired by some of the bridge's first users. Similarly, the brickwork of the voussoirs and lower piers is prominently jointed or 'Rusticated', another fashionable building effect.

But erosion has increasingly damaged the structure. Despite major repairs in 1955 (directed by George Pace), further deterioration occurred and in 2011 this Grade I listed structure joined the English Heritage 'at risk' register. Funding was secured however and while work remains to be done, most of the bridge superstructure has now been stabilised with resin injections.

A mason by trade, George Nicholson rose to become the Dean and Chapter's surveyor from 1771 until his death in 1793. His part in restorations to Durham Cathedral has been criticised (rather unfairly) ever since. Perhaps the elegance and popularity of Prebends' Bridge more than compensates for that.

Prebends' Bridge from the south.

Arch detail on Prebends' Bridge.

The Old Bridge, thrown down by the great flood in the Year 1771.

'Old' Prebends' Bridge before destruction in 1771. (Edis Collection, reproduced by kind permission of Durham University Library)

16. Assembly Rooms

Standing amidst grander company halfway along the North Bailey, this unusual building is a genuine hidden gem. It has two different façades, which conceal several distinct phases of construction history.

Built before 1750 when they advertised 'musick' concerts, the rooms were attended by Durham's fashionable elite. Mainly used for public balls and celebrations, the venue was directed by Messers Watt and Wetherell in the 1830s when Captain Ellis was Master of Ceremonies. Fine panelling and a period ceiling have survived inside what today is the university theatre's auditorium. Decorative plasterwork and a string of 'modallions' or small block-shaped brackets also remain within the ceiling's historic cornice.

Following an era of relative grandeur and then decades as a dancing academy, the old Assembly Rooms were given a new lease of life. Entrepreneurial tradesman Thomas Rushworth, who lived in nearby Saddler Street, demolished much of the former 'dancing rooms' in 1890 and replaced them with the Assembly Rooms Theatre designed by his architect brother, William Rushworth (1849– 1940). Judging by a contemporary sketch it had a grand classical entrance with painted-glass windows below a three-bay façade. Still extant, the upper section is built in red brick and framed by Doric pilasters (shallow, flat-faced columns.)

Above left: Double façade of Assembly Rooms in North Bailey.

Above right: Restyled Assembly Rooms when officially reopened in October 1891. (Drawing by Andrew Dodds)

It also has a Dutch gable, a design element used by Rushworth in several schools after his appointment as Durham County Council's education architect in 1904.

Operas and plays staged by the Assembly Rooms soon gave way to 'talking pictures' however, and in 1909 the structure was adapted again, becoming Durham's first cinema. Initially successful, its fortunes dwindled after the owner's death and the building became university property in 1930. Two decades later, after serving as headquarters for the university's Officer Training Corps, the old rooms took on their present appearance and returned to their theatrical past. The entrance was replaced with a vaguely art-deco foyer and above its austere concrete canopy were metal-framed 'Crittal' windows, a feature particularly associated with post-war modernism. Stylistically confusing though it may be, this building encapsulates the cathedral city's long history of entertainment. Major refurbishment, costing more than £2 million, is currently being carried out by the PH architects partnership. When complete the theatre will stage a combination of student and professional productions.

17. Haughton House

Haughton House is a splendid example of Baroque domestic architecture. Built in the 1720s for the prestigious Eden family, it is a highlight of the two baileys, credited by Pevsner to be Durham's 'best streets'.

Offset from the street for effect, the house stands out amongst more polite Georgian buildings in the South Bailey and is approached by an almost processional flight of stairs above the basement floor. The wide doorway is protected by a flat bevelled hood supported by three brackets which are decorated with stylised acanthus leaves, an architectural motif widely favoured in the Baroque period. Exuberant and even exhibitionist, this style was becoming unfashionable in the early eighteenth century but the Eden town house, though more restrained, was influenced by some of its characteristics.

Big and imposing, the building has three and a half storeys including a spacious basement level. Distinctive voussoirs were set above 'sliding box' sash windows, a seemingly exclusive English innovation developed during the seventeenth century. Seven bays wide, the house has a projecting central section with prominent cornice and an attic with round mouldings above. Extensively refurbished in 1996, the street façade is built in brick but clad with superior stone and each level apart from the basement is heavily rusticated. Wide gaps are deliberately left between the sandstone blocks to create horizontal linear patterning – a 'banded' type of rustication intended to emphasise the building's mass and convey an impression of strength.

The ostentation continues inside. Although most of the original interior has gone, the Eden building contains one of the city's best historic staircases. Sympathetically restored in the 1970s, it presents a dramatic single flight and displays the finest-

Below left: Baroque façade of Haughton House in the South Bailey.

Below right: Haughton House staircase.

quality woodcarving. There are Corinthian column-shaped newel posts, Doric spindles or 'balusters', and familiar acanthus leaf decoration on the tread sides.

After changing hands in the nineteenth century, the Eden town house became a school before acquisition by the present university owners in 1912. Renamed after Haughton Castle, Northumberland home of the Cruddas family who were major benefactors to St John's College, it now provides a suitably impressive administration and reception centre for students and visitors. The college crest, 'Fides nostra victoria' (Our faith is our victory), hangs above the doors.

18. Bowes House

This extended town house has been associated with the Bowes since the fifteenth century when Sir William Bowes held property on the site. Firmly established in the ranks of Durham's gentry, the family went on to become major coal owners. The mercurial Sir George Bowes (1701–60) was a long-serving MP for County Durham.

Bowes House has a complex story deeply woven into the South Bailey's history. Initially a defensive zone between the castle's circuit of walls, the bailey became home to cathedral servants and minor officials who lived in generally humble tenements. Over time they were rarely demolished completely, but often enlarged, or built over and later 'beautified' by their increasingly wealthy occupants.

John Lound, the bishop's 'temporal advisor' in the 1430s, was an early participant in this, acquiring tenements on the site later to become Bowes House. Lound's subsequent building development, known as 'Loundhouse', was afterwards purchased by Dean and Chapter registrar and lawyer Thomas Kyng. He seems to have amalgamated the various property holdings (houses around a vennel with stables behind) between 1592 and 1598.

But the modern history of Bowes House was effectively begun by Cuthbert Bowes when he obtained the lease of No. 4 South Bailey around 1689. Described at his death in 1715 as a 'Durham City Gentleman', he commenced fashionable home improvements to his residence. An impressive staircase in the mid-section of the house has been attributed to his time. Painted black and dog-legged, it has classical spiral or 'barley sugar' balusters and a flat handrail.

Bowes' successor, the Earl of Strathmore, continued the work in greater style with what is said to be the bailey's finest room. Now called the Tristram Room (after Victorian botanist Henry Baker Tristram), it has a gilded rococo ceiling and ornate woodwork with a 'bolection' or projecting frieze above the door.

Following the Bowes' departure at the close of the eighteenth century, their house had other various notable occupants including the Hutchinsons of Egglestone Hall. Purchased by St John's College in 1910, it is now Grade II listed in three parts that stretch north to south along the bailey. An elongated façade masks a large section of the building's various stages of construction with a thick coat of 'harl', a cosmetic and protective lime render popular in the north.

Rendered front elevation of Bowes House.

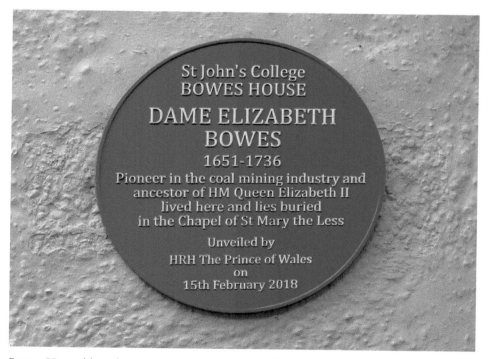

Bowes House blue plaque commemorating Dame Elizabeth Bowes (1651–1736). She was married to William Bowes, five times MP for Durham.

19. Hatfield College

Hatfield College is a further example of the university's successful adaptation of historic peninsula sites. Named after fourteenth-century Bishop Thomas Hatfield, it was the university's second college, established in 1846 and known as Hatfield Hall until after the First World War.

When purchased by the university from solicitor Walter Scruton in 1843, the North Bailey site, sloping down towards the river and close to the city's ancient east wall, was occupied by a disjointed group of buildings with a colourful past. They were originally related to a large house, possibly of medieval foundation and owned in the 1640s by the wealthy Heath family. Elements from John Heath's town house are said to be contained within the 'D Stairs' area of the modern college.

After conversion to the 'Folly Inn' and then the 'Red Lyon' coaching inn during the eighteenth century, the rambling property was purchased by the Scruton's for £2,000 in 1799. Although remodelled, the building's present left wing has retained its Georgian dining hall, lit by an east-facing 'Venetian' window. Classically Palladian, this tripart window-case has a central arched top flanked by shorter and narrower sidelights. Surrounding pilasters and an entablature complete the well-proportioned effect, providing a fashionable backdrop for the musical soirees once held in the Red Lyon. Georgian influence is also apparent in what is now Hatfield's adjacent dining room. Formerly the inn's card room, it has a shallow bow window and a marble chimney piece of contrasting colours.

William Jones's imposing façade of Hatfield College. Parts of the original old wing are on its left with Anthony Salvin's additions on the right.

Urgently required additions to the original buildings were first carried out by renowned Durham-born architect Anthony Salvin (1799–1881). Completed by October 1849, a three-storey 'A and B Stairs' accommodation block (known as the Melville building) displays his typically competent Tudor style and cost double the price of the entire site half a century before. A Gothic-style chapel at the North Bailey entrance designed by Revd J. F. Turner dates from 1854.

Student facilities were not markedly improved again until 1932 however, when 'C Stairs' were added. Replacing outdated parts of the old inn, the stuffily neo-Georgian new build was by Durham-based architect and antiquarian William Thorpe Jones (1864–1932). 'Bishop Hatfield's Hall' then continued to expand inside its North Bailey boundaries. The impressive Pace building, designed by Emanuel Harris, was built in 1950 while the Jevons Building (Bernard Taylor and partners) was completed in 1968.

20. Dunelm House

Dunelm House brought brutalism to Durham. Constructed between 1963 and 1966, it was designed as a Student Union and staff centre by American-born Richard Raine of the Architects Co-Partnership. Ove Arup was consultant engineer and the main contractor was John Laing.

Upper level and roof of Dunelm House from Kingsgate Bridge walkway.

Above: Rainwater drainage chains on Dunelm House.

Left: Framed by Kingsgate Bridge, Dunelm House is pictured here from the west bank of the River Wear.

After wartime plans to build on Palace Green were abandoned, a slightly less sensitive but more challenging riverside site at New Elvet was chosen instead. The structure that took shape there may have triumphed over the Wear gorge terrain, but has divided public opinion ever since.

Less visually dramatic now than when its gleaming white concrete was freshly laid, the Union building still presents something of a spectacle. A collection of shallow concrete boxes squat low at the Elvet street level and spill massively down to the riverside. Numerous windows, no more than slotted openings in blank façades, are discretely metal framed and have concrete mullions. From the riverside elevation they look out and up to the cathedral, a building which Dunelm's designers respected and never attempted to overawe.

Exposed concrete, a trademark of brutalist design, was used throughout the structure, forming almost everything from outer and inner walls to minor interior details. Even the roof, though originally specified to be zinc clad, was finally covered in large precast concrete tiles. A custom-made interlocking design, they sympathise with the surrounding roofscapes but not the rain of Durham City. Leaks and mould have been a long-term irritant and expense.

Built without a lift tower, Dunelm House relied on what was first termed by the architects as an 'internal street'. A continuous staircase, comprising a series of shorter flights, rises through the building. Unconventional perhaps, it links the structure's five main levels and unifies the design. Praised as an innovatory concept when first built, it has since come to represent (along with failing concrete and the faulty roof) the impractability of Dunelm House.

With repairs estimated by the university to cost over £14 million, the building is now under threat of demolition. This was compounded by its failure (unlike the

Grade I Kingsgate Bridge which accompanies it) to gain listed status. But it has many supporters and there is now an active campaign to save what is Durham's most controversial and modernist landmark.

21. Kingsgate Bridge

Connecting Dunelm House to the peninsula, the Kingsgate footbridge was completed in 1963. Ove Arup and Partners won the commission but Newcastle-born Arup became its driving force. With a small budget of £35,000, he ingeniously fulfilled his brief and delivered a functional and what many agree is an aesthetically pleasing structure.

It bridges the 350-foot-wide Wear valley in minimalistic style with a trough-like walkway, 10 feet wide and fabricated in two precast sections of reinforced concrete. Specialist building contractor Holst and Company (today part of Vinci PLC) produced and assembled the bridge's concrete components. White cement mixed with Shap Pink aggregate, a resilient Cumbrian stone, is particularly noticeable on the parapet's moulded round handrails. Sand blasting gave texture to exposed concrete surfaces and the platform sidewalls were imprinted by wooden shuttering, which the concrete was poured into. Overall, Arup's specified material has weathered well, acknowledged in 1993 by the Concrete Society's certificate for 'Outstanding Performance'.

Kingsgate Bridge from the east bank of the River Wear.

Above: Expansion joint in Kingsgate Bridge.

Left: Bust of Ove Arup (1895–1988) on Dunelm House at the east end of Kingsgate Bridge. It is a copy of the original by Diana Brandenburger, which was stolen in 2006.

Slender concrete piers, on cylindrical bases embedded in each riverbank, support the 300-ton weight of Kingsgate Bridge. Like giant inverted compasses, they form wide 'V' shapes at the tops, giving the bridge an angular presence. But they were also instrumental in the construction process, allowing each half to be built independently and opposite each other, causing less disruption and eliminating the need for expensive cross-river scaffolding. Keenly watched by Arup and his project manager John Martin, the two sections were steadily winched together, swinging on single-use bearings built into the conical bases. Though not entirely original, it was a perfectly tailored solution, epitomising Arup's concept of 'total design'. Distinctive cast-bronze expansion joints lock the structure in place.

Sir Ove Arup was a renaissance man of the building world. A combination of engineer, architect and philosopher, he earned an international reputation. Although probably best known for his work on the iconic Sydney Opera House, Durham was never far from his heart. Kingsgate Bridge was always a favourite and his ashes were scattered from its deck after his death in 1988.

22. Former Saddler Street Post Office

Durham's first purpose-built post office was opened on Saddler Street in December 1880. Before then the city was served by a few 'receiving offices' run by salaried postal agents (until the introduction of postboxes in the mid-nineteenth century) and there were other small post office premises, mostly inside shops. But this was a time of rapid expansion for Britain's post office and as the organisation grew, its buildings became grander.

Although a site in Gilesgate was initially considered, Saddler Street's central location proved more popular. Local tradesmen contributed £500 to the cost and the new main office was built on the site of the former Golden Lion Hotel.

Architect James Williams (1824–92) designed the building to impress as well as provide an important public service. Two storeys high and four bays wide, it was built in neoclassical style from brick and polished local stone. Doric pilasters separate the first-floor windows while above them is a distinctive full-length frieze patterned with 'guilloche', a French term associated with delicate classical detail. Grecian motifs also enhance window transoms and the projecting roof cornice, which originally read 'Post Office' in bold lettering. Although that is now removed, the accompanying royal crests and monograms remain.

During his career as an architect for the government's Office of Works, James Williams designed more than thirty post office buildings, several in the North East. Unsurprisingly, they share some design features. An open balustrade, for example (which appears to be his architectural signature), is prominent on the Saddler Street façade.

Post office interiors were all broadly similar however, determined more by function than artistic flair. Saddler Street's ground-floor hall was spacious and well lit, and had a long mahogany counter. Telegrams were written downstairs and sent upstairs by 'pneumatic lift' while letters were delivered, sorted and despatched behind the public hall. Closed as a post office when the new Claypath branch was built in 1927, this handsome building became an Employment Exchange and much later a betting shop. Part of it is now occupied by an Italian restaurant.

Saddler Street's former main post office. Storage vaults from the demolished Golden Lion Hotel remain beneath the building.

23. Town Hall and Guildhall

Civic buildings have stood in Durham's market place since the late medieval period. The Guildhall, positioned on the left of today's complex range of town hall structures, was rebuilt by Bishop Cosin in 1665, superseding the 'Tollbooth', a stone building erected around 1535. This was stated by nineteenth-century historian Eneas Mackenzie to have 'apartments behind it for public festivals' and these were once known as the 'Old Town Hall'. The Guildhall and adjoining Mayor's Chamber underwent further reconstruction in the mid-eighteenth century and an artist's impression from the 1820s suggests a building of classical style. Designed by local architect John Bell, it had a two-storey Palladian façade, a projecting central window and balcony, and a stylish roof cupola.

Between 1848 and 1851 however, Philip Charles Hardwick significantly remodelled and extended the existing market place site, creating a new indoor market and providing more space for a City Council which had been enlarged after the 1835 Municipal Corporations Act. London-born Hardwick (1822–92) modernised the Guildhall and added a spacious new public hall to the rear.

Opened on 29 January 1851, the new Town Hall was described in the *Durham Advertiser* as a 'beautiful structure' and the architect's designs were congratulated to be 'in correct taste'. Hardwick's Guildhall, restyled in a restrained Gothic Revival manner, was an important element in this. Built in sandstone and ashlar, it features a triptych of tall windows with elaborate tracery and chamfered drip moulds above them surmounted by a partially battlemented parapet. Complementing the Guildhall, the remaining Town Hall frontage is built in Perpendicular Tudor style.

This Victorian pursuit of fashionable antiquity continues in Hardwick's main hall. Concealed behind the market square façade, it was influenced by London's

Civic buildings and entrances to the indoor market hall on the west side of Durham Market Place.

Above: Guildhall façade and balcony.

Right: Town Hall interior with its distinctive hammer-beam roof.

Westminster Hall and like that medieval masterpiece albeit much smaller, has a remarkable hammer-beam roof. Made of oak, the open framework has ornately carved cross-timbers supported on carved corbels. Gas lamps originally hung from 'Gothic' brackets manufactured by the Potter ironworks company of London. They were designed by Hardwick to enhance the grandeur of a hall that is 72 feet long, 36 feet wide and 52 feet from floor to apex of the exposed rafters.

24. St Nicholas' Church

Durham's market place church is a Victorian building that occupies a medieval site. The original church is thought to have been built in the early twelfth century, during the era of Ranulf Flambard, one of Durham's great 'builder bishops'.

The early St Nicholas', depicted in drawings and a rare photograph, appears almost unrecognisable. Although facing the market place as it does today, it had a buttressed nave and chancel with a battlemented square tower to the west. Interior north and south aisles were divided by what an eighteenth-century antiquarian described as 'blunt pointed arches' and the heavy north wall was probably incorporated into the city fortifications, extended around the church after 1315. There were once graveyards to the building's front and rear and burials inside from a comparatively wealthy parish that had close ties with Durham's numerous craft guilds.

Despite this, the church was recorded to be 'very ruinous' in 1803 and half a century later was beyond repair. Market place improvements had led to the removal of the front churchyard and shortening of the chancel's east end before the building was completely demolished in June 1857.

Built close to the original foundations, the new St Nicholas' was opened with great ceremony on 21 December 1858. Estimated to have cost £3,600, the church was designed by James Pigot Pritchett Jnr, a York-born architect who practised in Darlington for over half a century. Won in an 1854 competition, St Nicholas' was an early ecclesiastical commission and though Pritchett (1830–11) went on to design many more, Pevsner regarded it amongst the best.

Much more imposing than the previous structure, the new church was constructed in Decorated style, imitating a phase of Gothic architecture lasting from around 1290 until 1380. Elaborate tracery was a particular characteristic of this period, and the windows of St Nicholas' are freely 'reticulated' with mesh-like swirls of stone ribs.

Interestingly, the church steeple was an afterthought. Omitted from the initial plans on cost grounds, it was only added to the specification after it was paid for by vicar George Townshend Fox. When finally erected, 160 feet high and costing £400, it was the only one in the city. Extensive reordering, including moving the altar to the nave's south wall, was carried out in 1982 by ecclesiastical architect Ronald Sims (1926–2007). Grade II listed, this Anglican church is often open.

Right: St Nicholas' Church viewed from the south end of the market place.

Below: North side of St Nicholas'. Its architect, J. P. Pritchett Jnr, worked in collaboration with his brother-in-law John Middleton between 1852 and 1854.

25. Former National Provincial Bank

A Pevsner favourite, this dignified bank commands the south side of Durham's market place. Banking agencies were active in Durham City from the 1770s at least and local partnerships such as the Durham Bank and the Northumberland and District Bank were established during the early Victorian period. Failures amongst many provincial banks like these however led to amalgamation or acquisition by larger, London-centred organisations and construction of Durham City's National Provincial branch began in 1876.

The impressive new premises were designed by Warwickshire-born John Gibson (1817–92). As official architect for the National Provincial Bank of England from 1864, he was responsible for over forty branches nationwide, several in the North East including Stockton, Sunderland and Newcastle. All were styled in Gibson's influential classical manner, described by historian John Lloyd Booker as 'the backbone' of Victorian bank architecture.

Gibson's Durham bank is a superb example. Calm and confidently Palladian in style, the three-storey and seven-bay frontage was built from 'Stainton' stone, quarried near Barnard Castle in County Durham. Approximately 60 feet wide, the façade is articulated by ascending quartets of projecting columns framed by rusticated piers. Tuscan order on the ground floor and composite above, the attached pillars convey

The conservatively classical frontage of John Gibson's National Provincial Bank (now NatWest).

a sense of strength and stability – imperative for any financial institution. A pierced balustrade and elegant detailed cornices add to the prestigious appearance.

Eating and toilet facilities for clerks were provided in the basement while senior staff had rooms and offices on the two upper floors. The spacious ground-floor banking hall originally had high-quality mahogany fittings and a floor covered with 'encaustic' or inlaid tiles. Made from different-coloured clays, this type of decorative tile was known from the medieval period and revived during the nineteenth century.

Described in the *Durham Advertiser* as a 'splendid building', the new bank (main contractor Mr R. Sanderson of Durham) began trading on 7 February 1878. It remains a bank and a powerful statement of Victorian commerce.

26. The Gala Theatre and Cinema

Named to acknowledge Durham's annual celebration of coal mining heritage, the Gala was opened in January 2002. Occupying former derelict land at the head of Claypath, this new theatre and cinema complex was built as a centrepiece of the Millennium Centre development scheme.

It serves the purpose well. Simple but bold, the structure fills most of Millennium Square's north-eastern side. A long boxy profile is broken by a tower at the square's entrance and two smaller ones towards the river. One of these,

The Gala's river-facing elevation.

Gala entrance on Millennium Square.

cider clad, is the 'fly tower', directly above the stage and used to house rigging and machinery. The other marks the auditorium below, designed for an audience of 500. Such functional elements are now routinely undisguised in contemporary architecture. But the auditorium's angled roof, painted red, is held by some to disturb an otherwise engaging outline (particularly when noticed from afar).

Costing around £15 million, The Gala was part of a design by London-based practice MacCormack Jamieson Prichard and was preferred to three alternative proposals in a competition. Lead architect David Prichard, inspired by a range of structures from local vernacular to the Festival Hall, created a building described by architectural critic Edwin Heathcoat to be in a 'restrained modern style'.

The Gala, constructed largely of smooth-finished stone and rendered surfaces, has a traditionally aligned interior with stalls and circle facing a separate proscenium stage. An orchestra pit, able to accommodate forty musicians, is part of a versatile auditorium that can be refigured into a single space for exhibitions or similar public functions. Glass also features prominently. On the main north-west-facing elevation, a raked glazed wall, reminiscent of a huge ship's bridge, allows cross-river views.

After MJP Architects (as they are now known) were established in 1972 they gained a reputation for their work in historically significant areas. Consequently, although certainly modern, the Gala does not ignore its traditional and ancient surroundings. It has overhanging roof eves and domestic-looking 'ribbon' windows. And the Gala's tall east tower, watching over the entry to Millennium Square, is near the site of the medieval Clayport Gate, demolished in 1791.

27. Former URC, Claypath

This once-neglected church faces the street on the north side of Claypath. Dissenting religious groups have met and conducted services here since the late seventeenth century and a restrained and polite Presbyterian chapel, built in 1751, remains behind the main building.

Enlarged in 1850, the red-brick chapel still proved inadequate for Durham's growing Nonconformist congregation and was succeeded by a new church under the banner of the Congregationalists who had merged with local Presbyterians in 1821.

Costing around £5,000 and constructed from snecked sandstone quarried in Hebburn-on-Tyne, the Congregational Church was designed by Henry T. Gradon (1855–1917). Durham born, he worked as an architect in England and South Africa before returning to the city around 1880. A Congregationalist himself, he designed many other buildings in and around Durham, notably the Miners' Hall at Redhills.

Written off by Pevsner as 'large and crudely Gothic', Gradon's new church was actually welcomed by the Durham press as 'a handsome little place of worship' after opening in June 1886. In Decorated Gothic style, the building has dogtooth mouldings surrounding both main doors with a quatrefoil window above them. There are raised decorative bands with gargoyles on the 115-foot-high belfry and a distinctive central column at pavement level. Of pink granite, it has an acanthus leaf capital. More significantly however, a large five-light window on the front elevation has a version of geometric or 'bar' tracery, a French innovation adopted into English decorated architecture of the thirteenth century.

The church interior was arranged to follow the pattern of Nonconformist worship. Preaching was an important component of this and a congregation of over 400 could be seated in the building's main body with a further ninety in a gallery which faced the pulpit.

A United Reformed church after 1972, the building was disused by the turn of the century. Acquired by Durham's Anglican Evangelical denomination in 2011 and renamed Christchurch, it has since been restored and furnished with a new balcony. As part of a £1million project by OMI architects, the Victorian church is now permanently linked with the adjacent chapel and is again part of Durham's religious and communal life.

Below left: Claypath's Former Congregationalist and United Reformed Church, now Christchurch.

Below right: Acanthus leaf capital at the front of Former Congregationalist Church.

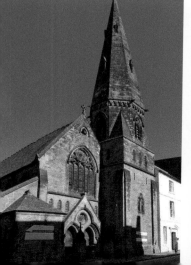

28. St Antony's Priory

Dedicated in 1990, the chapel at St Antony's Priory was Durham City's first such religious building since the Reformation. It is also the most unconventional. Clearly modernist, it contrasts but does not clash with the adjoining Victorian main house. Virtually unseen from the steep Claypath street, the chapel's shard-like octagonal tower rises above the slope and there are thrilling views of Durham Castle and Cathedral to the south-west.

Yet the building's use of traditional materials also softens its angular profile and helped win it Durham Council's annual built environment award. Constructed with warmly toned Dunhouse sandstone, the exterior has a faceted or rusticated finish, sympathising with its historic neighbourhood. Welsh slates cover the tower's steeply pitched roof and green Westmorland slates were used for interior floors and benches

The unconventional exterior profile of St Antony's Priory.

Octagonal interior of St Antony's Priory. The timber altar was constructed in 1990 by Ken and Jenny Grant.

St Antony's adjacent Victorian villa, modified in 1898 by Durham City architect George Ord (1850–1925). Its attractive gardens contain fragments of medieval stonework from the original St Nicholas' Church, demolished in the 1850s.

on the tiered seating. Perhaps symbolically, the chapel is placed at the centre of a trinity of levels, with a sacristy and garage occupying the other two floors. Unifying the design, a glazed external corridor links the new chapel with the old house and outbuildings. Built on farmland in 1850 as Bellevue House, this was adapted by George Ord in 1898 to become a vicarage for the nearby church of St Nicholas.

The priory chapel was commissioned by the Society of the Sacred Mission, an Anglican religious order established in 1893. As well as St Antony's, purchased in 1985, the society has a primary establishment at Willen, Milton Keynes, with foundations in South Africa and Australia.

The new chapel was the work of architecture graduate Sarah Menin (now a distinguished theorist and practitioner) supported by Newcastle University's architectural project office. Within the interior octagon, Dr Menin's design delivers a contemporary and harmonious place of worship with an unusual altar table as its central focus. Resting on a rough-carved natural stone base, it has a polished circular top with decorative metal insets. Light and space are maximised, and the chapel is well illuminated with a range of inset clerestory windows, some angled to reflect the building's geometric form.

A modern outpost in an area of traditional church design, St Antony's is an ecumenical centre of spirituality. Accessible to private and community groups, it is a 'peaceful oasis' to all who spend time there.

29. Leazes Place

This collection of buildings is included here as one of Durham's best-surviving examples of mid-nineteenth-century domestic architecture.

'Leazes', a relatively common term, may refer to the open pasture and garden plots which once lay around Claypath. Despite a sloping terrain, the area was ripe for development. At that time Durham's overall population was expanding only modestly but the nearby peninsula's congested and insanitary centre had the county's highest mortality rate.

Built around 1840, Leazes Place is Grade II listed and comprises a pair of terraces facing each other across a narrow street still paved with cobbles. Although not built as a single development, the design is visually consistent and the two-storey houses appear almost indistinguishable. All have sober red brickwork, tidily laid in English garden wall bond. This type, alternating three rows of stretcher or longside bricks with one of headers or shortend bricks, became widespread in the North East from the late eighteenth century and was often used in Durham City.

Apart from those with an elevation on Claypath, the houses have two bays, processing orderly along a north–south axis. Although built in the first years of Victoria's reign, they are imbued with Georgian and Regency style. Sashed windows have retained their small glazed panels and thin glazing bars alongside doors with six panels and overlights (some also with glazing bars). Their doorcases are

East Terrace of Leazes Place. Vertical mortar lines between houses indicate separate phases of construction.

Above left: West side of Leazes Place.

Above right: Railing detail on Leazes Place.

particularly refined. Most are plain Tuscan pilaster style while others are fluted and incised with Greek key decoration. A bracketed Victorian gas lamp and ornamented boot scraper catch the eye, but while some are missing, the street's spear-headed railings are perhaps more significant. Like the doorcases they guard, they may have been inspired by the Greek Revival designs of local architect Ignatius Bonomi.

Apart from a few skilled artisans, Leazes Place was occupied mainly by prosperous members of Durham's middle class. A doctor had his surgery in No. 12 and No. 4 became a girls' school in the 1850s. These attractive terraces, described by Douglas Pocock as a 'visual delight', are today shared by long-term residents and a transient student population.

30. Former Mechanics' Institute

Now occupied by a restaurant business, this impressive building on Claypath was erected as a Mechanics' Institute. Such establishments flourished from the 1820s and in the latter part of the century there were over 1,000 across Britain. Rooted in the technical demands of the Industrial Revolution, they provided lectures and reading rooms to educate and inform the working man.

Durham's Mechanics' Institute began in temporary premises on Saddler Street in 1825. Their committee (including founder member Ignatius Bonomi) spent years gathering support and funding for a permanent base and encouraged the availability of a wider range of non-scientific topics such as art, history, and French.

After disagreements about its less central Claypath location, a plot was eventually purchased and the new institute's foundation stone was laid on 30 March 1849. Designed by Bonomi, the building cost £750 and was in use by

Former Mechanics'
Institute on the south
side of Claypath.

December of that year. But despite the two-storey structure being reported as 'no small ornament to the town', Bonomi distanced himself from the project. Still objecting to the site, he credited the completed structure largely to the efforts of clerk of works Thomas Dickons.

Today the former institute strikes a dignified note on a rapidly changing Claypath street. Sturdily built from sandstone ashlar, the classical three-bay façade is articulated by Tuscan-style pilasters. Coarsely finished, banded rustication covers the ground floor down to a basement plinth, while the upper level is smooth with a pronounced cornice. Though much of the original interior is lost, fragments of moulded cornice work remain. An entrance hall, library and caretaker's accommodation once occupied the ground floor while there was a lecture room above. A reading room, added shortly after the main building was finished, was accessed through an arch.

Thriving in the 1850s, the Durham Mechanics' Institute declined in popularity as the century wore on. Despite many becoming more community orientated, most institutes could not compete with the expansion of alternative recreational opportunities. Free libraries and in particular the 1889 Technical Instruction Act (giving control to education authorities), accelerated their general demise. Obtained by the Oddfellows Society of Durham around 1900, the Claypath building was subsequently hired out. By 1925 it was a Ministry of Employment Exchange and later became J. W. Wood's auction rooms.

31. Kepier House

Established in 1852 as the Durham County Penitentiary for women, Kepier House in lower Gilesgate is one of the city's less publicised buildings. Described in the *Durham Advertiser* as a purpose-built refuge for the 'homeless and houseless female outcast', the original structure was designed by County Surveyor John Howison (1811–88).

First built in Britain at the beginning of the nineteenth century, female penitentiaries became more widespread during the moralistic Victorian era. Aimed to rescue and safeguard the so-called 'fallen women', these institutions employed disciplined programmes of work and instruction, preparing their voluntary inmates for a return to virtuous society. After a Northumberland 'House of Mercy' was constructed at Newcastle in 1831, powerful voices were raised to ensure County Durham had a similarly worthy establishment.

Founded on 'self-sustaining principles', the penitentiary was an entirely charitable foundation. In July 1851 the publicly donated building fund reached £300, allowing the purchase of a 1-acre field in Gilesgate. Relatively isolated at that time, the site was deliberately selected to keep it from the public eye. Furthermore, to keep unwanted callers out and inmates in, it was also to be enclosed with a tall boundary wall spiked with broken glass (which failed to prevent Mary Thompson absconding in September 1874).

Roofed in December 1851 by contractor Mr Punshon, the building was completed in August the following year. Architect John Howison was secretary to

Kepier House (former Penitentiary), now restored as part of Kepier Court student accomodation.

Gilesgate Penitentiary from a contemporary depiction by Joseph Bouet (1791–1856).

the penitentiary committee and had been a supervisor on the 1849 construction of Newcastle's High Level Bridge. He delivered the Gilesgate project within his budget estimate of £1,900. An early drawing shows the large two- and three-storey gabled house in tranquil surroundings overlooking Durham Sands. Deliberately plain, the new penitentiary was initially praised as a 'spacious edifice', its cruciform plan intended to simplify any later extensions. Inmates mostly carried out seamstress and laundry duties. A new washhouse was added in 1909 before the local authority and latterly Durham University took charge of the site.

Refurbished by Robertson developments in 2017, the still-recognisable former penitentiary is now a central part of Kepier Court, one of Durham's latest student 'villages'.

32. Kepier Hospital Gateway

This gatehouse is a picturesque reminder of Kepier's medieval hospital. More accurately termed the Hospital of St Giles of Kepier, the original almshouse for hospitality and 'the keeping of the poor' was built further south in Gilesgate around 1180 in the episcopate of Bishop Hugh le Puiset (or 'Pudsey'). He transferred the establishment to the present riverside site, after the first hospital was destroyed in 1144 during a violent Anglo-Scottish contest for the Prince Bishop's throne.

The new location was well chosen. Quarry stone was within easy reach and abundant fish, a dietary staple, could be trapped on the adjacent weir. (Kepier's place name is a derivation of Old English for 'fish' and 'weir'.) Just as importantly

Above: Kepier Hospital's impressive gateway. (Image by Tony Robinson)

Right: The White Bear Inn (formerly the Heath Mansion) shortly before demolition. (Drawing by Andrew Dodds after 'Durham in Old Photographs' by June Crosby)

perhaps, the replacement hospital lay on a pilgrim's way which led to Cuthbert's shrine around 1 mile to the south-west.

Noted in the official listing as a 'Great Gateway', Kepier's entrance block is a Grade I Scheduled Ancient Monument. It was built for prestige and defence by Bishop Richard de Bury between 1333 and 1345. Although badly weathered like much of the masonry, a crest above the doorway may display his insignia.

Constructed from coursed sandstone blocks, the imposing structure has two storeys and three bays with a central, triple-arched opening. Directly above the exterior pointed arch is a banded frieze ornamented with a barely visible 'quatrefoil' motif (four linked circles). The arched passageway is rib vaulted with ceiling bosses, also now almost unrecognisable. Rooms flanking the main entrance, one with a spiral stairway and another with a large fireplace, were used by hospital gatekeepers.

Comprising a chapel (dedicated to St Mary and All Saints), infirmary, hall and dormitory for a master and thirteen 'brethren', the hospital buildings were probably ranged around a courtyard. Fundamental change followed the Reformation however, as the hospital and its estate fell into private hands. Suppressed in 1545, Kepier was then acquired by Sir William Paget, then John Cockburn before it was purchased by London merchant adventurer John Heath. His family retained the gatehouse (one of them living in it) and built a stone and brick mansion over parts of the hospital foundations. All that stands now of Heath's grand house, a pub when demolished in 1892, is a stylish Elizabethan arcade.

33. St Giles' Church

St Giles' was the first hospital chapel to be built in County Durham. Dedicated to the Greek-born patron saint of the sick and disabled, it was consecrated by Bishop Flambard in June 1112 and may have been damaged in 1144 by forces loyal to Scots chancellor William Cumin during his failed attempt to seize the bishopric. A simple font and more certainly the nave's north wall, still pierced by original round-headed openings, are survivors from that time. It is also believed that the first building was of cruciform plan with a central tower or crossing.

In a commanding position overlooking the city, the chapel became the parish church of St Giles' Borough and the focus of Gilesgate's emerging community. Bishop Hugh Pudsey granted a charter to the 'vicus' of Gilesgate and rebuilt its church between 1153 and 1195. Pudsey's reconstructed chancel has elongated windows with pointed arches, in typically late Norman or 'Early English' style. Rebuilding continued with the demolition of Flambard's west wall, eventually

St Giles' Church viewed from the south-east.

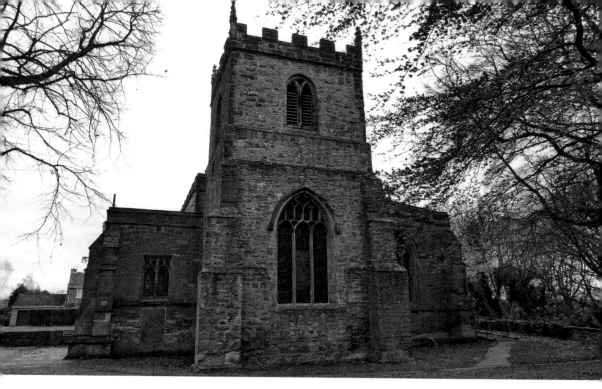

Above: West end tower of St Giles'.

Right: Recently restored effigy of John Heath on his tomb in St Giles'.

replaced with a square tower. Commenced in the early thirteenth century, it has four stages and was completed around 1414 during the term of Bishop Thomas Langley. He refurbished parts of it and added ground-floor windows. A local landmark, it terminates the building's west end with its crenellated parapet and corner pinnacles.

St Giles' was the subject of extensive nineteenth-century alterations and additions, not all universally welcomed. In 1824 for example, when architect Philip William Wyatt removed inappropriate sash windows, their replacements were derided as 'pretentious' and 'would be perpendicular'. However, though further repairs were carried out in 1843, it was generally agreed that more urgent restoration was required. Fortunately ignoring recommendations for complete demolition, the church authorities listened to public protest instead and began renovation and enlargement. Carried out between 1873 and 1876 by Austin and Johnson of Newcastle, the works included the addition of a north porch, south aisle, organ chamber and vestry as well as external buttresses. Perhaps inevitably, an unappreciated Wyatt east window was replaced with a 'correct' example of five lights and perpendicular tracery. The church contains a remarkable wooden effigy of landowner John Heath, who died in 1591.

34. Vane Tempest Hall

Built as a militia headquarters, Gilesgate's Vane Tempest Hall is now the last of its kind in County Durham. Traditionally formed during episodes of national emergency and eventually becoming army reservists, local militias can trace their history back to pre-Conquest times. Durham's militia was first raised in 1759, commanded by regimental colonel Lord Henry Vane. Based at Barnard Castle with a complement of 369 balloted men, the force was reorganised by the 1852 Militia Act. Reformed into two divisions the following year, one regiment remained in Barnard Castle while the other was transferred to Durham City as the 2nd, or North Durham Militia.

Initially quartered in Church Street, the North Durham's eventually went to Gilesgate Moor. Costing £300, a 2-acre part of Gilesgate's 'Holywell field' was purchased from the Dean and Chapter. Concerns had been raised about the site's capacity and the hazards of ammunition storage, but contracts for the militia's new buildings, accommodating storerooms and quarters, were awarded by July 1864. Although disrupted by weather and the bankruptcy of the main contractor, the new headquarters were ready a year later.

Designed by County Surveyor William Crozier, the structure is suitably grand and martial (probably in deference to George Vane Tempest, Lord Londonderry, the militia's most powerful supporter). Sometimes referred to as 'a mock castle', the two-storey building has a distinctive octagonal corner entrance turret with a battlemented parapet and decorative arrow slits below it. Built from snecked sandstone, the exterior is 'L' shaped with five bays and three dormer windows to each wing. Also with blind arrow slits, the dormers are edged with coping stones and finished with vertical end pieces or 'kneelers'. This arrangement is repeated on a larger scale in the main gables, which have fleur-de-lis roof finials. Originally serving as the drill hall, the building's right wing has a hammer-beam roof and the central stairway has retained its simple but functional iron handrail.

Incorporated with the newly formed Durham Light Infantry, the former militia left their Gilesgate barracks for Newcastle in January 1884. Later an isolation

Above: The bold exterior of Vane Tempest Hall.

Right: Vane Tempest Hall's dedication plaque to the 2nd Durham Militia.

hospital, then used by Volunteer Corps, Scout groups and air-raid wardens, Vane Tempest Hall today is a valuable asset for local businesses and the Gilesgate Community and Welfare Association.

35. Masonic Hall

Old Elvet's Masonic Hall is one of Durham's more idiosyncratic architectural statements. A marked contrast to the plain brick of its predominantly Georgian neighbourhood, it was constructed largely from high-quality dressed ashlar quarried locally at Brasside.

Squeezed between an eighteenth-century pub and early nineteenth-century houses, the Masonic building has two storeys and a central attic. Described in contemporary newspaper reports as 'early geometrical gothic', its narrow façade combines freely adapted Gothic influences with elaborate Masonic detail. Windows are pointed, of one and two lights and particularly on the first floor have a version of 'plate' tracery, a pre-thirteenth-century window form. Dominating the building's front is an acutely angled entrance arch supported by short and closely coupled pillars. With classical pretensions, they are made from polished red Aberdeen granite and have richly decorated cushioned capitals.

Symbols of Freemasonry are incorporated throughout the structure. Roundels above the large bay window are crammed with Masonic devices and the eye of Providence or 'all seeing eye', its brow oddly distorted, is carved into the apex of the portico arch. Surmounting that is a five-pointed star made from intersecting triangles, another common Masonic emblem. And flanking that are 'rampant' lions, vigorously grasping shields of the Duke of Zetland, Order Grand Master, and John Fawcett, Provincial Grand Master.

Below left: The Masonic Hall's highly ornamental façade on Old Elvet.

Below right: Detail of Masonic Hall's entrance canopy.

Main function room
with five-light window
in Masonic Hall.

Amongst other features, the interior is noted for a wide staircase, described as 'bold handsome' (sic) by the *Durham Advertiser* in 1869, and a spacious banqueting hall, which has an open hammer-beam roof over 30 feet high. Beyond the triple stairway, its heavy outer string pierced with Masonic geometry, the hall is illuminated by an extensive five-light window on the east gable. Now floodlit at night, it has 'cathedral tinted glass' with designs representing the Freemasons' five points of Fellowship.

Established in 1763 as the Marquis of Granby Lodge, Durham's Masons met first in a local tavern. Based in Old Elvet's Chapel Passage from around 1815, they afterwards raised £1682 from Masonic balls, bazaars and donations to finance their move further along the street. Designed by architect and lodge member Thomas Charles Ebdy (1839–1911) and built by contractor Thomas Punshon, their new hall was ceremonially dedicated on 22 December 1868 and fully opened a year later. As well as Masonic functions, the hall is now used as a wedding, conference and party venue. Described by Pevsner as 'fortunately small', this fascinating building is nevertheless worth its place in the Durham streetscape.

36. Former Shire Hall

This Victorian and Edwardian extravaganza dominates Old Elvet's south side. A monumental structure, it was a resounding expression of Durham County Council's growing municipal strength. Formed in 1889, they deflected some protests about cost and pressed ahead with plans for a substantial new headquarters on Old Elvet.

Sunderland-based Harry Barnes and Frederick Coates were runners-up in the competition to build it, but were controversially awarded the contract for the new Shire Hall and were criticised as 'more or less unknown' by a more established but disgruntled London practice.

In late 1895, after plans and sketches were displayed in local shop windows, the tendering process was completed and construction began. The foundation stone was laid by the Lord Lieutenant in April 1896, and what was hailed as Durham's 'local Parliament' opened in July 1898.

Built by Sunderland contractors David and John Ranken at an estimated cost of almost £14,000, the Shire Hall was constructed largely of terracotta bricks from the Ruabon works in Wales. Comparatively inexpensive and hard-wearing, this material was a popular choice in the late nineteenth century and became the bright-red face of many High Victorian structures.

In Baroque Revival style, the hall's main façade on Old Elvet was over 200 feet long when first built. A copper dome on clustered shafts, compared to the style of Buckingham Palace architect Aston Webb, features prominently and the building's decorative wrought ironwork was supplied by J. W. Singer of Frome in Devon. Nine bays wide, the basement and two-storey layout could accommodate 100 councillors in the ground-floor debating chamber and committee rooms. Noticeably less assertive, a three-bay suite of education offices, designed by William Crozier Jnr and also built by Ranken's, was added in 1905. Redundant in 1963 however, the entire structure was then sold to Durham University.

Big, bold and (though mellowed) still red, the old Shire Hall has offended many architectural critics. Thomas Sharp called for its demolition in 1938 and Pevsner later snarled at it in print. Empty since 2012, it has now reopened as a luxury hotel. Again a local collaboration, design work was by Durham's HL architects and final refurbishment by Brims of Sunderland.

Above left: Now 'Hotel Indigo', the red-bricked former Shire Hall dominates Old Elvet's south side.

Above right: Copper-sheathed dome of former Shire Hall.

An early twentieth-century postcard view of Durham's old Shire Hall. The banded sandstone extension of 1905 is seen on the far left. (Reproduced by kind permission of Durham County Record Office D/DW1/7 (68)

37. Elvet Methodist Church

John Wesley first visited Durham in 1742 and there have been Methodist places of worship in the Elvet area since 1770. The present church in Old Elvet, opened in November 1903, was the third and largest to have been built.

An imposing church rather than a plain chapel, the new Wesleyan building was a big departure from its 1807 predecessor in the cramped nearby street of Chapel Passage. Yet by the late nineteenth century, at local and national level, Methodism was seeking to raise its profile. The new church demonstrated the prosperity and taste of Durham's Methodists as well as their ability to raise a building as fine as its Anglican counterparts.

Although set well back from the main street, the Elvet structure challenges the scale of the adjacent Shire Hall. The 110-foot-high church spire towers above the neighbourhood.

Built on the site of a former private school, the new church and adjoining Methodist classrooms cost around £10,000, much of this secured before construction began. Laid out on an unconventional north–south axis, which suited the wedge-shaped plot, it was designed by Bradford architect and active Wesleyan William James Morley (1847–1930). While better known for factories

Old Elvet's Methodist
Church and range of
ancillary buildings
viewed from the south.

and mills, Morley's practice enjoyed Wesleyan patronage, completing many
churches for them in what the *Dictionary of Scottish Architects* describes as 'a
rather repetitive Gothic style'. (Stockton's Methodist church on Yarm Road for
example, near contemporary with Durham, is almost a mirror image.)

Nevertheless, Morley's ecclesiastical designs were grand and relatively
expensive. The Elvet church was built in Perpendicular Gothic Revival fashion, its
façades well detailed and faced with rusticated or 'pitched' stonework (chipped to
resemble natural rock). Contrasting ashlar dressings and moulded jambs delineate
the Gothicised front widow, which is large, has five lights and complex tracery.
A capacious interior provided accommodation for 500 worshippers, while the
gallery allowed for a further 150.

Extensive interior alterations were completed in 1995 and although Elvet's
Wesleyan congregation has now reduced to around 200, it is the largest on
Durham's Methodist circuit.

38. Former Assize Courts

Durham's historic Assize Court, now a Crown Court, is the city's largest Georgian
structure. Its building history, beginning in 1809, is a tale of four architects.
Irish-born Francis Sandys drew up the first plan for new courts and a 'House of
Correction' intended to replace Palace Green's old courthouse and the squalid
gaols in the North Gate and beneath Elvet Bridge.

Although the new court was open by 1811, accusations of poor design and
unsupervised workmanship ineptly done led to Sandys' dismissal and a lawsuit
that destroyed his reputation. His successor, experienced prison designer George
Moneypenny, fared little better. Moneypenny demolished a good deal of Sandys'
work and continued building, but was also replaced in 1814 after further
disputes and delays.

Durham's majestic former Assize Courts. After reordering its interior, William Crozier was appointed by an impressed Northumberland Council in 1877 to carry out similar improvements in Newcastle's Moot Hall, even though they had their own architect and surveyor.

Assize Courts around 1834 (from Mackenzie and Ross' *An Historical, Topographical and Descriptive View of the County Palatine of Durham* – Vol 2).

Durham's young County Surveyor Ignatius Bonomi then salvaged the project and consolidated his career. After more remedial work and at a total cost of just over £112,000, the court and prison complex behind it was completed by Bonomi in 1821. The impressive Assize Court frontispiece, possibly a combined Sandys-Bonomi design in the neoclassical manner practised by both, crowns the head of Old Elvet Green. Of high-quality ashlar, its austere façade is dominated by a projecting central portico articulated by four 'giant' (two-storey-high) columns. Plain Tuscan, they are 'engaged' or partially buried in the wall surface, a feature common to ancient Italian architecture. With a temple-like pediment above them and a wide flight of steps below, they form a grand yet intimidating entrance to the courts of justice.

The original interior, indisputably planned by Bonomi alone, was completely remodelled in 1869 by County Surveyor William Crozier (1829–1905). Reported in the *Builder* magazine to have received 'warm commendation', the new court was lavishly appointed. Granite cement floors were inlaid with the Maw Company of Worcester's vivid encaustic tiles and the ceilings were deeply panelled and coved.

Crozier's complicated internal scheme, incorporating Tuscan columns and arched wall pilasters, may now seem rich and repetitive for some modern tastes but this detracts little from the significance of a powerful edifice, erected to convey the authority of Britain's nineteenth-century state.

39. St Cuthbert's RC Church

St Cuthbert's Church was built for the Catholic congregation of what was known as 'Popish Elvet'. Catholicism doggedly endured in this district after the Reformation and there were two 'recusant' private chapels in Old Elvet during the eighteenth century. As religious tolerance advanced however, Catholics were allowed more public forms of worship and work on a new church and presbytery commenced in April 1826.

Opened a year later on 31 of May, St Cuthbert's was built by a Mr Jackson and designed by Ignatius Bonomi (1787–1870). Of Italian parentage and trained in London, Bonomi established himself as an accomplished regional architect after becoming County Durham's Bridge Surveyor in 1813. Best known for eclectically styled country houses and domestic buildings, this versatile professional also built and restored a number of Anglican and Catholic churches.

Constructed from smooth ashlar in Perpendicular Gothic style, St Cuthbert's, though not big, was originally even smaller. Described in Whellan's 1856 local

Above left: St Cuthbert's from the east with its Presbytery on the far left.

Above right: St Cuthbert's stained-glass window by Harry Clarke (1889–1931).

directory as 'a neat stone structure', the building was enlarged in 1869 when parish priest Edward Consitt added a Lady Chapel (between north wall buttresses) and an East Tower. Gothic in three tiers, it was poorly built and needed subsequent reinforcement. Grafted on, it seems to have reused stone from the earlier east end but repeated Bonomi's design, seen clearly on his sketched plan, of an arched and hood-moulded entrance door.

Beyond that the interior space has remained essentially intact. Like Bonomi's later and larger Catholic church in Sunderland, summarised by Michael Johnson as 'a classic preaching box', St Cuthbert's is simply proportioned. Displaying characteristic late Georgian regularity, its shoebox-like body is 70 feet long by 30 feet high and wide. Below a flat panelled oak ceiling the walls are lined with boards patterned with a Gothic motif, which is echoed across the east end balcony.

The interior furnishings have greatly changed however. Amongst several reorderings a new altar was installed in 1910 and nave windows replaced between 1931 and 1932. Most cherished of these is one by Irish stained-glass artist Harry Clarke depicting northern martyrs and saints.

St Cuthbert's was Durham's first Catholic church after the Reformation and is a monument to the historic courage and resilience of Old Elvet's Catholic community.

40. Hallgarth Barns

Secreted away behind the prison just off Hallgarth Street, this group of buildings is unique in Durham City and the surrounding region. While there seems no solid evidence to prove it, they are known traditionally as 'Tithe Barns', a collection and storage area for crops owed as payment to the church. What is certain however is that they are rare survivors from the medieval priory's Elvethall Manor (or Hallgarth) estate farm, used to supply the nearby cathedral's monastic community with agricultural produce. Wheat, barley and oats were cultivated on farmland within sight of the peninsula and any surplus was sold off to the local population.

Dating from the mid-fifteenth century, the major buildings now visible on the site comprise two large former barns and a smaller structure at right angles to them. This compact two-storey building at the west of the range is now known to have been a granary, used possibly for holding farming equipment as well as grain. Once workaday, now picturesque, its ashlar and sandstone rubble ground floor projects into the old farmyard and has an arched doorway for farm wagon access. A Grade II* listed building, it has a rendered brick and wood upper level with vertical timbers or 'studs' fixed narrowly apart to form 'close-studded' walls. Richard Halme is recorded to have fabricated the jointed and pegged roof truss, much of which is unfortunately now concealed.

Equally well-crafted woodwork is more clearly seen in the roof of the adjacent barn. Also constructed from oak, it is another superb example of late medieval

Above: Hallgarth Granary with barns on the right.

Below: Interior of former barn, now used as a prison officers' club.

carpentry skill. Supported on stone corbels, it has high-set vertical posts forming two corridor-like apertures in what is termed a 'raised aisle' truss structure.

After the easternmost and largest building (probably the 'Great Barn' referred to by cathedral archives) was seriously fire damaged in the mid-twentieth century, both structures were restored and reroofed with pantiles, a lighter red-clay substitute for the original stone covering. These important former barns are now used as a social club and offices by the Prison Service. Despite some repairs however, the even more remarkable granary next to them still remains on Historic England's 'at risk' register.

41. Victoria Inn Public House

Now one of a number of listed public houses in Durham City, the Victoria Inn was built in 1899. Central to the New Elvet district, it also served coal miners from nearby Elvet Colliery until the pit closed in 1908.

Erected on Hallgarth Street, the hostelry was the work of Carlisle-born Joseph Oswald (1851–1930). Educated in Newcastle, he was trained as an architect there by his father Septimus. Probably best known for large Newcastle schemes such as the Central Arcade and the Newcastle Breweries headquarters in Percy Street, the Joseph Oswald and Son partnership also designed a number of regional pubs,

The Victoria Inn and later extension on Hallgarth Street with Church Lane on the far left.

One of the
Victoria Inn's
colourful interiors.

many for the Newcastle Breweries Company. They completed over 130 pub commissions between 1876 and 1939, most built between 1890 and 1914 when Joseph ran the firm.

Originally called the Victoria Hotel, this wedge-shaped building was described in the *Durham Advertiser* as 'handsome and commodious'. It replaced demolished cottages and an earlier tavern dating from 1890 (said by its manager to be no more than a 'tumbler box') which stood on the east side of the present site.

Brick built on a plinth of buff sandstone, the two-storey Victoria Inn has mullion (vertically divided) windows on the ground floor. All above are sash windows apart from two small transom (horizontally divided) types over the north end door. Horizontal banded courses of darker stone help relieve the façade's expanse of red brickwork, as do the contrasting sandstone dressings around windows and doors. An embossed date plaque above the north entrance, featuring a rather youthful-looking Queen Victoria, also adds some interest.

But the pub's interior is much more likely to capture the imagination. Largely unaltered due to the efforts of long-standing owner Michael Webster, the building has retained its unusual configuration and many Victorian fittings. It has elaborate fireplaces, an ornamental bar and a tiny screened-off snug with 'Family Department' etched in glass on the door.

While lacking the exuberant glazed terracotta cladding or 'faience' used by Oswald on some of his more expensive projects, the Victoria Inn more than compensates for that in charm. Known locally as the 'Vic', it has been deservedly termed 'Durham's most original pub'.

42. St Oswald's Church

This arresting building may have been founded centuries before the cathedral. Dedicated to Northumbria's saintly King Oswald, it occupies a dramatic position opposite the peninsula in Elvet, said to be the ancient 'Aelflet ee' or 'Swan Island', which is identified in early sources as a probable Christian site. Apart from suggestions of a Saxon burial ground and some pre-Conquest fragments however, there is no more substantial proof.

Fortunately, St Oswald's later medieval history is somewhat less obscure. Built of stone and ashlar, the present structure was mother church to the 'Old Borough' and the 'Barony of Elvet', an extensive parish endowed to the cathedral priory by Bishop William St Calais in 1083. With a prominent west tower, long nave and chancel, this church (like many others) has been heavily remodelled and incorporates work from several historical periods. St Oswald's exterior is difficult to date accurately, but the oldest surviving part of the building is believed to be four bays of the interior's eastern arcade. Supported by characteristically rounded arches and circular piers, it was constructed around 1195. Contemporary with them is the chancel arch, its simple plant motif or 'waterleaf' capitals unscathed after a fourteenth-century rebuilding phase that included widening of the north aisle.

Further additions in the following century, mainly the clerestory and tower, made the church increasingly grand. A hammer-beam roof was also installed. Constructed from oak, it was described by antiquarian Robert Surtees to be inscribed in gold with the name of William de Catton, vicar between 1411 and 1414. Even more radical alterations were made in the nineteenth century. A series of restorations, necessary because of presumed mining subsidence from the adjacent Elvet Colliery, were carried out between 1834 and 1883. Directed most

Below left: St Oswald's Church and its ancient churchyard, said by Professor David Rollason to be a possible site of Durham's pre-Conquest 'White Church', where St Cuthbert's body lay for a short time.

Below right: St Oswald's stained glass by Ford Madox Brown.

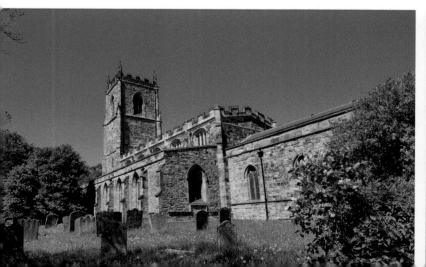

notably by Ignatius Bonomi in 1834 and Hodgson Fowler in 1864, a vestry was added and the south aisle and chancel were entirely rebuilt. Early features including most of the nave's fine roof were lost but the church also made significant gains. As part of Fowler's reconstruction, a splendid stained-glass window, designed by artist Ford Madox Brown in collaboration with the William Morris Company, was set into the tower. In muted tones, it depicts episodes from Oswald's life. Another window by Clayton and Bell of Newcastle shows Fowler with a plan of the church. St Oswald's survived a serious fire in 1984 and continues to be one of Durham's most intriguing if underappreciated churches.

43. The Palatine Centre

The Palatine Centre is Durham University's new flagship building. Replacing an outdated and increasingly impractical Old Shire Hall site, it has become the university's administrative headquarters and provides a diverse range of student services as well as housing a new law school in the east wing.

Named to acknowledge the authority of Durham's Prince Bishops, the Palatine complex took four years to build and cost £50 million. Officially opened in October 2012 by distinguished scientist Sir Paul Nurse, the project was overseen by the Cundall Building Services consultancy and the main contractors were Laing

The Palatine Centre on Stockton Road.

Palatine Centre's 'internal street' with *The Sphere of Redemption* by English artist Fay Pomerance (1912–2001) in the foreground.

O'Rourke. It was designed by locally based architects Space Group in conjunction with the PH Partnership.

Largely an interplay of curved glass and timber, which marches awkwardly down the south side of Stockton Road, the Palatine rises high above a low plinth of fine stone blocks. Four large rectangular bays project from the main street façade, which is articulated by an avenue of laminated wooden beams. Like giant spider legs, they arc down from the upper levels and though not supporting the entire structure, brace the extensive roof elements above them.

Interior space revolves around a long central atrium. Glass roofed, it illuminates the building naturally and links the internal accommodation, functioning as an 'internal street' (a concept encountered earlier at Dunelm House). Palatine's street may be entered at the west end where, extending the sinuous motif, a semi-rotunda contains a reception area, restaurant and bar.

The sustainability of natural materials was at the heart of the structure's design specification. They are used throughout the building, particularly on the exterior cladding and roofs covered with red cedar shingles. Similarly, the building is equipped with solar heating systems and rainwater recycling tanks.

Yet despite such environmental credentials, the Palatine's radical appearance has ruffled important architectural feathers. Lambasted by Durham's prestigious Civic Trust as 'monstrous' and 'alien', the centre was also nominated for (but did not win) a rather less coveted 'Carbuncle Cup' award.

44. The Ogden Building

Durham University's most visually striking building to date is part of the Ogden Centre for Fundamental Physics. The second building on the Lower Mountjoy Physics site to be dedicated to former Durham graduate and philanthropist Sir Peter Ogden, this new structure on South Road was opened in March 2017.

Built for astronomy and cosmology research, it was designed by avant-garde architect Daniel Libeskind and his New York-based 'Studio Libeskind' practice. Through major commissions such as the extension to Berlin's Jewish Museum and his leading role in the Twin Tower site redevelopment, Polish-born Libeskind has established a worldwide reputation for thought-provoking and sometimes controversial work. His Scottish Larch-clad building in Durham displays aspects of both.

Like a distorted Rubik's cube, its complex shape unfolds when approached uphill from the junction at Stockton Road. Erected on a former car park, the large-scale structure essentially comprises a series of angular forms, which are stacked, twisted and slotted together. Its exterior terraces and courtyards are clever and useful but interior illumination and 'openness' were the building's stated design imperatives. East and west façades are punctuated with rows of windows while the north, deliberately skewed to face the cathedral, has a tilted wall of glass. Skylights above a central atrium perform a similar function, flooding the building's three levels with natural light. The centre's offices spiral around the perimeter with communal areas and a conference room placed at the core of a structure intended by Libeskind to be public art as well as practical architecture. Many would agree and though some find

The astonishing Ogden Centre viewed from South Road.

Public art as well as architecture – north aspect and main campus entrance to the Ogden Centre.

his 'deconstructivist' style disorientating, the Ogden building has met with general approval. Winner of several international prizes, it was also declared a 'clear winner' of the City of Durham Trust's 2016 architectural award.

Costing over £11 million (with substantial donations from the Ogden Trust and the Wolfson Foundation), the project was overseen by English architect Wendy James and engineered by the Arup consultancy. The Ogden Centre's cutting-edge design complements the scientific institution it was built for.

45. St Aidan's College

Ranked amongst Britain's best post-war architects, Sir Basil Spence (1907–76) was commissioned in 1960 to design St Aidan's College, south of the river on Windmill Hill. New accommodation was required for Durham's growing number of female undergraduates, known as 'home students' since 1895 and reformed as St Aidan's Society in 1947.

Though not the university authority's immediate preference, Basil Spence had delivered his Coventry Cathedral masterpiece and was then conveniently working on projects in Sunderland and Newcastle. But his modernist scheme for Sussex University, begun in 1959, swung the Durham appointment in favour of Spence and his John Glover and Peter Ferguson partnership.

Above: St Aidan's student accommodation at left, extending towards the dining hall on the right.

Below: St Aidan's dining hall and ornamental pond.

On a superb site overlooking the peninsula, St Aidan's was one of Durham's first 'Hill Colleges'. Principal Miss Ethleen Scott, champion of the new building's construction, cut the first sod in December 1962 and though incomplete, it was occupied by the first of its 200 students in October 1964. Officially opened in June 1966, the 'golden brick' and concrete structure was broadly admired, welcomed by contemporary student magazine *Castellum* for example as 'unconventional and striking'.

Influenced by Le Corbusier's simple geometrical style, the St Aidan campus is set around a wide central space or courtyard. Described to be generally dull by a respected architectural critic, low-rise student accommodation flanks each side. The east wing is in two separate rows, while the west curves dramatically towards a taller main communal area dining hall, St Aidan's most successful feature. Very similar to Spence's Sussex design, its reinforced concrete and brick-clad frame has three monumental, fully glazed bays. They have an antique, vault-like motif, repeated inside, which make a distinctive bar and dining area, providing spectacular cathedral views.

Yet Spence's original blueprint for St Aidan's was never fully implemented. Always regretted by the architect, sufficient funding for an elaborate chapel to the south, said to represent the 'star of knowledge', was never raised. Male students were admitted to the college in 1981 and since then, while St Aidan's has been considerably extended, Spence's buildings stand largely undisturbed.

46. St Margaret's of Antioch

Originally part of St Oswald's parish, St Margaret's was built around 1160 as a chapel of ease for residents of Durham's 'Old Borough', a district just to the west of Framwellgate Bridge. Grade I listed since 1952, the church was dedicated to the early Christian Saint Margaret, who was born and martyred in what today is modern Turkey. A niche above the Tudoresque north porch door, reached by steps from Crossgate's hilly street, shelters a Victorian statue of St Margaret's patron saint.

Probably without a tower, the earliest church is believed to have been a simple form of chancel and nave with an arcaded south aisle. An original clerestory window remains above the south arcade. A north aisle was added slightly later when the chancel was enlarged. Its arcade, contended by medievalist Bertram Colgrave to be contemporary with late twelfth-century elements of St Oswald's, is another Norman survivor. The chancel arch, now distorted but probably saved from total collapse by modern buttressing, is also likely to date from the time of Bishop Pudsey (1153–95).

The south aisle was reconstructed around 1343, followed by more major alterations in the next century. Building the new west tower in particular would effectively confirm the status of a building declared an 'independent parochial chapel' in 1431. In four stages, the coursed sandstone tower has a battlemented parapet but uncommonly lacks buttresses.

Improvements and internal repairs due to subsidence were completed in 1794 but subsequent Victorian restoration was much more radical. Carried

Above: South elevation of St Margaret's of Antioch Church.

Left: Unusual south arcade capital in St Margaret's.

out between 1865 and 1880, the extensive works were largely to the design of Nottinghamshire-born Charles Hodgson Fowler (1840–1910). From an ecclesiastical family, this prolific architect was a pupil of Sir George Gilbert Scott and established his Durham practice in 1864. Described as a 'committed Gothicist' by architectural historian Graham Potts, Fowler believed his church restorations were an act of Christian faith as well as sensitive architecture. Amongst his other alterations to St Margaret's, he widened the north aisle, added the vestry and rebuilt both porches.

Open regularly, this attractive and well-preserved church has a notable memorial to Sir John Duck, mayor of Durham in 1680. It also has a curious 'zoomorphic' or animal-like carving in the south arcade.

47. North Road Methodist Church

North Road's Bethel (House of God) was built in 1853 as a chapel for New Connexion Methodists. This strand of Wesleyanism emerged from Staffordshire

North Road Bethel Chapel with railway viaduct in right background.

Upper-floor box pews and organ in Bethel Chapel.

in 1797 and Durham's adherents established a small chapel at Old Elvet in 1828. Described by the *Durham Advertiser* as 'handsome and commodious', the new and much larger structure was also an important addition to the development of the 'new' North Road, initially called King Street, which was begun in 1831.

Constructed from squared sandstone blocks on a tall rusticated basement, the chapel was estimated to have cost over £2,000. Congregation member and local businessman Joseph Love made a significant contribution to this and played an active part in the lengthy search for a suitable location. Elvet and Claypath were eventually ruled out and North Road may have been favoured partly because of its potential to attract converts in an increasingly populous and predominantly working-class district. Around 800 people could be accommodated in the new building's galleried interior. Its foundation stone was laid on 4 May 1853 and despite several accidents during construction, it was opened in August the following year.

The Bethel was erected by Durham builder and magistrate Robert Robson to a remarkably assured design by his teenage son, Edward Robert Robson (1835–1917). After training in the Newcastle office of John Dobson and with George Gilbert Scott in London, Robert junior (usually referred to as E. R.) embarked on his own distinguished career. Clerk of works at Durham Cathedral from 1858 until 1864, he afterwards moved to Liverpool and then the capital where he made his name as a far-sighted designer of numerous schools for the newly formed London School Board.

More than an austere 'preaching box', E. R. Robson's North Road Bethel was a neoclassical-styled demonstration of rising nonconformist status in Durham. Entered through an elevated Ionic porch, the main road façade has an imposing triangular pediment with an entablature resting on giant Doric pilasters. Major internal alterations, carried out in 2010 by Bishop Auckland architect John Niven, have retained much of the building's essential character while adapting it for modern liturgical and community use.

48. Redhills – Durham Miners' Hall

Durham's most outstanding late Edwardian building stands in landscaped gardens on Flass Street. Often called the 'Pitman's Parliament' but resembling a stately home, the Miners' Hall was built as a new headquarters for the Durham Miners' Association. Formed in 1869 and with a membership of around 200,000 at the beginning of the First World War, this trade union organisation had outgrown their original North Road base, designed by Thomas Oliver of Newcastle and opened in 1876.

Plans for a larger building, accommodating considerably more mining delegates, were submitted by local architect H. T. Gradon in late 1913 and speedily approved by the council. Building commenced shortly afterwards on a site at the foot of Redhills Lane already familiar to Gradon. A school designed by him in 1906 on the same plot, then owned by the nuns of St Thomas's Convent, was never built. But his subsequent effort was more successful and despite the wartime situation, the

Redhills – Miners' Hall. (Image courtesy of Andy Dowson at the Durham Miners' Association)

Debating chamber of the Miners' Hall. (Image courtesy of Andy Dowson at the Durham Miners' Association)

new Miners' Hall and offices were officially opened by D. M. A. Secretary Thomas Cann, on Saturday 23 October 1915. Two pairs of adjacent semi-detached villas for union officials were also erected in the £30,000 scheme.

Described by the *Durham Advertiser* as 'palatial', the Baroque-style hall was partially constructed from red, high-quality brick. The south-facing façade is 160 feet wide and stands on a plain ashlar plinth, deeper and containing basement windows on its downhill half. Gradon's symmetrical design has a classical projecting entrance bay with a grand Venetian window and open pediment on its central axis. Two copper-sheathed domes, one capping an Ionic porch and a larger more ornate one above it on the roof, are an acknowledgement of the first Miners' Hall on North Road and an indication of how far advanced was its successor. A marble and Derbyshire stone vestibule leads to the debating chamber, the building's principle feature. This large oak-panelled room was known as 'the chapel' to the delegates who filled its pew like benches.

H. T. Gradon's finest achievement was sadly also his last. Illness prevented him completing the project and he died in 1917. Building work was finished by his assistant E. Rutherford with C. Groves of Chester-Le-Street, the main contractor. Seeking a new purpose since the coal industry's demise, the hall is now set to undergo restoration as a centre for culture, community and history, but it will always remain a memorial to Henry Gradon and a monument to Durham's coal miners.

49. Durham Railway Station

Perhaps not surprisingly, the architecture of Durham Station is usually ignored. Perched high above North Road with famously distracting city views, it was opened on 1 April 1857 for the North Eastern Railway. Built by Thomas Prosser, it was possibly adapted from a design by G. T. Andrews and was erected in conjunction with the eleven-arch railway viaduct, an impressive engineering feat by NER's Chief Engineer T. E. Harrison (1808–88).

Yet Durham's newest station was certainly not ignored by the local press. In May 1856, even before completion, the North Road building was criticised by the *Durham Advertiser* as 'neither very large, nor very handsome' and its exposed single platform was similarly condemned.

But remodelling carried out by Prosser between 1871–72 rectified some of that. Before his appointment as the NER's first company architect in 1854, Thomas Prosser (1817–88) was a pupil of Ignatius Bonomi and clerk of works on John Dobson's grand Central Station scheme in Newcastle. During a successful career with the NER, Durham was one of Prosser's more modest projects and its reconstruction was completed shortly before ill health forced his retirement in 1874.

Prosser's improvements included expansion of the site to provide a new north platform, waiting room and ancillary offices. But apart from replacing corner turrets with buttresses, he retained the original cruciform-plan main building,

Durham Station's Grade II listed portico.

Restored Victorian canopy on the northbound (down) platform at Durham Station.

using its Tudor and Gothic styling to flavour the rest of his redesign. The old main block has a battlemented central portico (mocked as 'a miniature apology' in 1856) with large Tudoresque openings. Prosser's newer range opposite is in a blander cottage style but has the same ground plan as the main block and is also built from coursed sandstone with ashlar dressings.

More significantly however, he erected canopies over the windswept platforms. Impressively engineered, the surviving north roof's cast- and wrought-iron trusses are supported by slim metal columns with leaf capitals. Their combination of lightness and strength in subtly applied Gothic style is assessed by railway historian Bill Fawcett as Prosser 'at his best'. In 2010, restored and with sympathetic modern extensions, Durham Station was at last judged to be large and handsome enough when it received the City of Durham Trust's annual award.

50. Crook Hall

Grade I listed Crook Hall is one of Durham's oldest secular buildings. Believed to date from the late thirteenth century, it was established as a manor house and farm in medieval 'Sydgate', less than a mile north of the cathedral. Peter de Croke was an early fourteenth-century resident after whom the manor may have been named.

In almost continuous occupation since then, this remarkable building mirrors centuries of changing architectural style and taste.

On rising ground above the River Wear, the hall is a diverse assortment of buildings, laid out on an approximately east–west axis. A three-storey house with sash windows and glazing bars forms the projecting west wing. Begun in 1730, this was remodelled shortly afterwards by the Hopper's of Shincliffe, creating the elegant Georgian structure seen today. One of its well-proportioned interior rooms is graced by a plastered ceiling relief of a dove and basket, symbol of the Hopper dynasty.

The family preceding them also left their mark. London attorney Christopher Mickelton purchased the estate in 1667 and over the next half century his successors erected what now lies at the centre of the Crook Hall range. Internal paint finishes, woodwork and a bull's eye window bearing the date 1671 are rare survivors from their Jacobean manor.

The adjoining medieval hall is even rarer. At the east end, it is reached through a 'screens passage' or corridor in the Mickelton's seventeenth-century extension. Once partly ruined, now restored, it has kept its minstrel's gallery and double curved or 'ogee' headed lancet windows. The influential Billingham family resided there from around 1372 until the mid-seventeenth century and modified the building for their own domestic use.

Southern aspect of Crook Hall with eighteenth-century house on left. (Image by Bill Dixon)

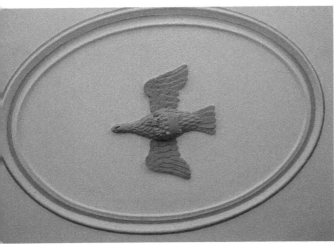

Above: Great Hall and Minstrel's Gallery in Crook Hall. (Image by Bill Dixon)

Left: 'Bird with a basket' ceiling plasterwork in Crook Hall. (Image by Tony Robinson)

Adaptations continued into the twentieth century when the conservation of Crook Hall became a major concern. Designed to be as historically accurate as possible, restoration and conversion of the hall's medieval and Jacobite core was carried out between 1983 and 1984. Costing around £110,000, this was supervised by Durham Cathedral's consultant architect Ian Curry. Still privately owned, Crook Hall and gardens retain an atmosphere of rural tranquility and are regularly open to the public.

Bibliography

Allan, G., *View of the City of Durham* (1824)

Boyle, J., *Guide to Durham* (n.d.)

Brickstock, R., *Durham Castle* (2007)

Brown, D. (ed), *Durham Cathedral: History, Fabric and Culture* (2014)

Clack, P., *Book of Durham City* (1985)

Crosby, J., Durham in Old Photographs (1990)

Crosby, J., *Ignatius Bonomi of Durham* (1987)

Green, A., *Building for England* (2016)

Green, L., *Building St Cuthbert's Shrine* (2013)

Hugill, R., *Castles of Durham* (1979)

Johnson, F. F., *Historic Staircases in Durham City* (1970)

Johnson, Margot., *Durham* (1991)

Johnson, M., *Sunderland in 50 Buildings* (2016)

Pevsner, N., *County Durham* (1990)

Pocock, D., *Durham* (1998)

Pocock, D., *The Story of Durham* (2013)

Potts, G., *Some Notes on Durham Architects* (2013)

Proud, K., *Durham City* (2003)

Richardson, M., *Durham City: Pictures From the Past* (2006)

Roberts, M., *Durham: 1000 years of History* (2003)

Roberts, M., *The Buildings and Landscapes of Durham University* (2013)

Tweedy, J. M., *Popish Elvet* (1981)

historicengland.org.uk/listing

The Building News and Architectural Journal

The Durham County Advertiser

The RIBA Journal

Acknowledgements

Many thanks to John Hayton and June Dodds for research assistance and proofreading, respectively. Andrew Dodds created the drawings and Durham University Library allowed me to photograph the Pace extension interior and supplied archive images as well as a current one of Cosin's Library. Friends and former work colleagues Bill Dixon and Tony Robinson accompanied me around Crook Hall and Kepier Hospital and kindly permitted me to use their images of the visit. Thanks also to Kate Barton of the Assembly Rooms Theatre, Revd Dr Nicholas Buxton at St Antony's Priory, Andy Dowson of the Durham Miners' Association and the staff at Durham Record Office. Special thanks above all to Graham Potts, Durham resident and retired senior lecturer in history at Sunderland University, who generously gave time to revisit the locations and comment on the drafts. His expert architectural insight and text corrections have been invaluable. Any remaining mistakes and misinterpretations are mine alone.